Workshop on Events and Stories in the News (EventStory 2018)

Santa Fe, New Mexico, USA
20 August 2018

ISBN: 978-1-5108-6914-1

EventStory 2018

Events and Stories in the News

Proceedings of the Workshop

August 20, 2018
Santa Fe, New Mexico, USA

Introduction

Welcome to the 2018 edition of the Events and Stories in the News Workshop (EventStory 2018), co-located with the 27th International Conference on Computational Linguistics (COLING 2018) in Santa Fe, NM, USA.

This workshop series aims at gathering together a multidisciplinary research community investigating technologies for representing and accessing events and stories from news as data structures. Events are one of the basic ontological constructs of human perceptions and stories are sequences of events with an internal coherence. Understanding both as data presents significant challenges that touch on semantics, natural language processing, knowledge engineering, artificial intelligence, human cognition and philosophy. A small but growing number of researchers are investigating various facets of that problem.

We received 17 submissions to this workshop, from which 10 were accepted for presentation. The accepted submissions display the links between events and stories, as well as show the breadth of the field; ranging from domains such as digital humanities and security to creating corpora and annotation schemes for events and storylines all the way to approaches and experiments to extract this information from text.

In addition to regular presentations and a poster session, the workshop will host a keynote by Professor Heng Ji (Rensselaer Polytechnic Institute). Following the success of last edition, we will host a new collective hands-on annotation session. Through the annotation task, we will work towards common definitions of core concepts for events and stories, and how to add them to common resources for annotating and evaluating events and storylines in an NLP setting.

We thank the members of the Program Committee for their timely reviews and all the authors for their contributions.

The Organising Committee.

Events and Stories in the News
http://eventstory.news

Organizers:

Tommaso Caselli, Rijksuniversiteit Groningen (NL)
Ben Miller, Georgia State University (U.S.A)
Marieke van Erp, KNAW Humanities Cluster, Digital Humanities Lab (NL)
Piek Vossen, Computational Lexicology & Terminology Lab, Vrije Universiteit Amsterdam (NL)
Martha Palmer, Department of Linguistics, University of Colorado (U.S.A)
Eduard Hovy, Language Technologies Institute, Carnegie Mellon University (U.S.A)
Teruko Mitamura, Language Technologies Institute, Carnegie Mellon University (U.S.A)
David Caswell, Reynolds Journalism Institute, University of Missouri (U.S.A)
Susan W. Brown, Computer Science Department, University of Colorado (U.S.A.)
Claire Bonial, Army Research Laboratory (U.S.A.)

Program Committee:

Alexandra Balahur, European Commission Joint Research Centre (IT)
Anne Bies, Language Data Consortium (U.S.A.)
Nate Chambers, US Naval Academy, (U.S.A.)
Jacob Eisenstein, Computational Linguistics Lab, Georgia Tech, (U.S.A.)
Ruihong Huang, Texas A&M University, (U.S.A.)
Mark Finlayson, Florida International University, (U.S.A.)
Robert Frederking, Carnegie Mellon University, (U.S.A.)
Erik van der Goot, European Commission Joint Research Centre (IT)
Martijn Kleppe, Koninklijke Bibliotheek (NL)
Bernardo Magnini, Fondazione Bruno Kessler (IT)
Roser Morante, Vrije Universiteit Amsterdam (NL)
Nasrin Mostafazadeh, University of Rochester (U.S.A.)
Vivi Nastase, Universität Heidelberg (DE)
Tim O'Gorman, University of Colorado (U.S.A.)
Octavian Popescu, IBM Watson Research Center (U.S.A.)
James Pustejovsky, Brandeis University (U.S.A.)
Georg Rehm, DFKI (DE)
Rachel Rudinger, Johns Hopkins University (U.S.A.)
Irene Russo, Istituto di Linguistica Computazionale "A. Zampolli" - CNR (IT)
German Rigau, Universidad del Pais Vasco (ES)
Tomohide Shibata, Kyoto University (JP)
Mihai Surdeanu, University of Arizona, (U.S.A.)
Xavier Tannier, LIMSI-CNRS (FR)
Ivan Titov, School of Informatics, University of Edinburgh (U.K.)
Sara Tonelli, Fondazione Bruno Kessler (IT)
Marc Verhagen, Brandeis University, (U.S.A.)
Laure Vieu, IRIT, Université Paul Sabatier (FR)
Lucie Vanderwende, Microsoft Research (U.S.A.)
Travis Wolfe, John Hopkins University (U.S.A.)

Invited Speaker:

Professor Heng Ji, Rensselaer Polytechnic Institute (U.S.A.)

Table of Contents

Every Object Tells a Story
James Pustejovsky and Nikhil Krishnaswamy...1

A Rich Annotation Scheme for Mental Events
William Croft, Pavlina Peskova, Michael Regan and Sook-kyung Lee........................7

Cross-Document Narrative Alignment of Environmental News: A Position Paper on the Challenge of Using Event Chains to Proxy Narrative Features
Ben Miller...18

Identifying the Discourse Function of News Article Paragraphs
W. Victor Yarlott, Cristina Cornelio, Tian Gao and Mark Finlayson........................25

An Evaluation of Information Extraction Tools for Identifying Health Claims in News Headlines
Shi Yuan and Bei Yu...34

Crowdsourcing StoryLines: Harnessing the Crowd for Causal Relation Annotation
Tommaso Caselli and Oana Inel...44

Can You Spot the Semantic Predicate in this Video?
Christopher Reale, Claire Bonial, Heesung Kwon and Clare Voss...........................55

Fine-grained Structure-based News Genre Categorization
Zeyu Dai, Himanshu Taneja and Ruihong Huang...61

On Training Classifiers for Linking Event Templates
Jakub Piskorski, Fredi Saric, Vanni Zavarella and Martin Atkinson.......................68

HEI: Hunter Events Interface A platform based on services for the detection and reasoning about events
Antonio Sorgente, Antonio Calabrese, Gianluca Coda, Paolo Vanacore and Francesco Mele....79

Conference Program

Monday, August 20, 2018

09:20–10:30   **Session 1:**

09:20–09:30   ***Welcome and Opening Remarks***

09:30–10:30   *Event Extraction and Tracking: Techniques and Challenges*
Heng Ji, Rensselaer Polytechnic Institute

11:00–12:30   **Session 2:**

10:30–11:00   ***Coffee Break***

11:00–11:20   *Every Object Tells a Story*
James Pustejovsky and Nikhil Krishnaswamy

11:20–11:45   *A Rich Annotation Scheme for Mental Events*
William Croft, Pavlina Peskova, Michael Regan and Sook-kyung Lee

11:45–12:05   *Cross-Document Narrative Alignment of Environmental News: A Position Paper on the Challenge of Using Event Chains to Proxy Narrative Features*
Ben Miller

12:05–12:30   *Identifying the Discourse Function of News Article Paragraphs*
W. Victor Yarlott, Cristina Cornelio, Tian Gao and Mark Finlayson

12:30–13:50   ***Lunch***

13:50–15:50 Session 3:

13:50–13:55 *An Evaluation of Information Extraction Tools for Identifying Health Claims in News Headlines*
Shi Yuan and Bei Yu

13:55–14:00 *Crowdsourcing StoryLines: Harnessing the Crowd for Causal Relation Annotation*
Tommaso Caselli and Oana Inel

14:00–14:05 *Can You Spot the Semantic Predicate in this Video?*
Christopher Reale, Claire Bonial, Heesung Kwon and Clare Voss

14:05–14:10 *Fine-grained Structure-based News Genre Categorization*
Zeyu Dai, Himanshu Taneja and Ruihong Huang

14:10–14:15 *On Training Classifiers for Linking Event Templates*
Jakub Piskorski, Fredi Saric, Vanni Zavarella and Martin Atkinson

14:15–14:20 *HEI: Hunter Events Interface A platform based on services for the detection and reasoning about events*
Antonio Sorgente, Antonio Calabrese, Gianluca Coda, Paolo Vanacore and Francesco Mele

14:20–15:50 *Poster session*

15:50–16:20 *Coffee Break*

Monday, August 20, 2018 (continued)

16:20–18:00   Session 4:

16:20–17:40   *Annotation Exercise*

17:40–18:00   *Discussion and Conclusion*

Every Object Tells a Story

James Pustejovsky
Computer Science Department
Brandeis University
Waltham, MA 02453
jamesp@brandeis.edu

Nikhil Krishnaswamy
Computer Science Department
Brandeis University
Waltham, MA 02453
nkrishna@brandeis.edu

Abstract

Most work within the computational event modeling community has tended to focus on the interpretation and ordering of events that are associated with verbs and event nominals in linguistic expressions. What is often overlooked in the construction of a global interpretation of a narrative is the role contributed by the objects participating in these structures, and the latent events and activities conventionally associated with them. Recently, the analysis of visual images has also enriched the scope of how events can be identified, by anchoring both linguistic expressions and ontological labels to segments, subregions, and properties of images. By semantically grounding event descriptions in their visualizations, the importance of object-based attributes becomes more apparent. In this position paper, we look at the *narrative structure of objects*: that is, how objects reference events through their intrinsic attributes, such as affordances, purposes, and functions. We argue that, not only do objects encode conventionalized events, but that when they are composed within specific habitats, the ensemble can be viewed as modeling coherent event sequences, thereby enriching the global interpretation of the evolving narrative being constructed.

1   Introduction

There has been significant research on the interpretation of events in text, particularly news articles (UzZaman et al., 2013; Pustejovsky et al., 2003; Aguilar et al., 2014). While identifying events and their participants has received much attention in the field, the construction of narratives, stories, scripts, and globally coherent relations between these events, is much more difficult and remains a challenging task (Chambers and Jurafsky, 2009; Rospocher et al., 2016). In this position paper, rather than focus on the semantics associated with event-denoting expressions in language, we discuss the contributions made by object participants in these events, and how these can influence or determine the global narrative event semantics of the text.

The semantic content of events is most often anchored to the matrix predicate of a sentence and the associated event participants, expressed as verbal arguments. Further complicating the interpretation of events is the fact that, while all entities are usually realized as nominal expressions, not all nominals are entities. That is, the participants in events can themselves be events, such as *Heavy rains resulted in flooding*, where both arguments are event-denoting NPs. In such cases, it is clear what role the NPs play in constructing a larger event-based narrative for the text. But there are many ways for a nominal expression to refer to an event, without denoting one. These are called *event-connoting* nominals. Examples include: *agentive nominals*, both occupational and social (dancer, baker, teacher, pilot, neighbor, friend); object *resultative nominals* (debris, mixture, waste, laundry); and all *artifactual nominals* (bread, coffee, desk, house, airplane).

We claim that, while the core structure of a narrative is largely formed through the composition of explicitly mentioned events, that are temporally ordered and constrained through discourse coherence relations, there is another latent narrative structure created from the events and activities associated with object-denoting participants in a text or image.

1

Proceedings of the Workshop on Events and Stories in the News, pages 1–6
Santa Fe, New Mexico, USA, August 20, 2018.

2   Linguistic Interpretation of Images

The body of work on text and image analysis relies on a number of techniques, e.g., semantic annotation of video; statistical classification for feature detection; heuristic, Markovian, and Bayesian methods for classification of composite events, among many others (Ballan et al., 2011). State of the art includes a variety of metrics to evaluate the robustness of caption generation systems (Anderson et al., 2016), event description (Young et al., 2014), and scene description (Aditya et al., 2015).

Previous work in visual semantic role labeling (e.g., Gupta and Malik (2015); Yatskar et al. (2016)) often involves determining the main activity and participants in an image or scene. In many cases, the activity is closely linked to one of the objects in the scene, and some canonical property of it. For example, in Figure 1 (taken from Yatskar et al. (2016)), we see two examples of a *spraying* event, both closely associated with one particular object in the scene—a spray can or a hose.

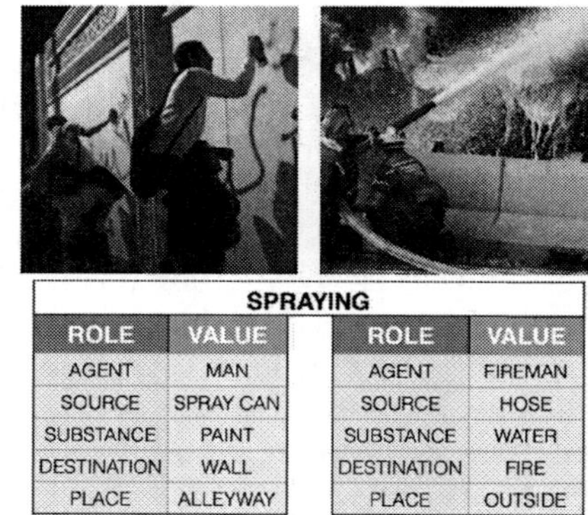

SPRAYING			
ROLE	**VALUE**	**ROLE**	**VALUE**
AGENT	MAN	AGENT	FIREMAN
SOURCE	SPRAY CAN	SOURCE	HOSE
SUBSTANCE	PAINT	SUBSTANCE	WATER
DESTINATION	WALL	DESTINATION	FIRE
PLACE	ALLEYWAY	PLACE	OUTSIDE

Figure 1: Spraying event with role labels, taken from Yatskar et al. (2016)

Both spray cans and hoses have canonical uses, which is to spray some substance (paint/water); knowing the canonical use of an object allows a human, as a reasoner, to infer what event or subsuming event is being depicted. Similar remarks hold for a tool such as a *chainsaw* (Figure 2a), independent of its role in an explicit *cutting* event (Figure 2b).

Figure 2: Latent Event (left) and Active Event (right)

In cases where an object is depicted as *violating* its canonical or typical use, the implied narrative becomes yet more interesting. The general "scenario localization" (Pustejovsky, 2013b) and particular types of textual or image narrative connotation can be either encoded or subverted by the presence and depiction/description of objects denoted/depicted within them: subverting the inherent narrative encoded into a particular object introduces a new narrative, vis-à-vis how the object came to be in the situation where is it depicted or described.

Take as an example the events associated with the object denoted by the artifactual nominal *plane*. The prototypical "fly" event can be broken down into the subevents "take off(a)," "translocation(a,b)," "land(b)," (encoded as Generative Lexicon's TELIC role). This forms a canonical *take off-fly-land* narrative associated with a plane. This lexically-encoded narrative can be left uninstantiated (a plane sitting in a hangar) or violated (by a *crash* event).

Figure 3: Airplane (left) and airplane debris in a field (right)

The image of debris in a field focuses this interruption or violation of the plane's canonical or typical purpose, as does a hypothetical image caption or snippet of prose narrative (e.g., "People walk among the debris at the crash site of a passenger plane near the village"), that presupposes the existence of the same debris and hence the event *crash* that interrupted the canonical narrative of the *plane*, causing it to enter into the situation where it (and the resultant debris) is described.

3   Habitats and Event-Connoting Expressions

In this section we introduce the specification for how latent event structure is encoded for entity types. Recall that there are three major types of event-connoting nominal expressions: (a) agentive nominals; (b) resultative nominals; and (c) artifactual nominals. Consider first the case of **artifactual nominals**. Following Generative Lexicon (GL) (Pustejovsky, 1995), such nominals are given a feature structure consisting of the word's basic type and its qualia structure. The latent event structure associated with an object is referenced through the qualia: e.g., a food item has a TELIC value of *eat*; an instrument for writing, a TELIC of $write$; a cup, a TELIC of $hold$, and so forth. Similarly, as mentioned above, the semantics for the noun *plane* carries a TELIC value of fly:

$$
(1) \quad \lambda x \exists y \begin{bmatrix} \textbf{plane} \\ \text{AS} = \begin{bmatrix} \text{ARG1} = x : e \end{bmatrix} \\ \text{QS} = \begin{bmatrix} \text{F} = vehicle(x) \\ \text{T} = \lambda z, e[fly(e, z, x)] \end{bmatrix} \end{bmatrix}
$$

While convention has allowed us to interpret the entire TELIC expression as modal, this is inadequate for capturing the deeper meaning of functionality, and this introduces the notion of a *habitat*. A habitat can be viewed as the environmental constraints, C, necessary for a latent event to be realized (Pustejovsky, 2013a). Assuming a dynamic semantics for how events are interpreted (Pustejovsky and Moszkowicz, 2011), we can say of an artifact, x, in the appropriate context C, that performing the action π will result in the intended or desired resulting state, $\mathcal{R}$, i.e., $C \rightarrow [\pi]\mathcal{R}$. That is, if a context C (a set of contextual factors) is satisfied, then every time the activity of π is performed, the resulting state $\mathcal{R}$ will occur. Hence, while the TELIC event for *plane* is *fly*, it is modal, and the preconditions for such an event must be satisfied, e.g., it has to be oriented properly, have fuel, it is air-worthy, etc., as well as be situated such that it can take off from a source, cruise in a trajectory, and land at a destination. An enriched lexical representation for such information of *plane* would involve far more operational and procedural knowledge than typically associated with the semantics of lexical items, going beyond the normal purview of qualia structure.

For this reason, in order to more richly represent this knowledge structure computationally, we are exploiting the modeling language VoxML (Pustejovsky and Krishnaswamy, 2016; Krishnaswamy and Pustejovsky, 2016), which was initially developed in the context of 3D modeling of language in "multimodal semantic simulations," wherein a computational system can render its interpretation of an event visually, for evaluation or to interact with a human. The VoxML equivalent of the above habitat structure, accounting for placement of the parameters within the embedding space $\mathcal{E}$ is given below:

$$(2) \quad \begin{bmatrix} \textbf{plane} \\ \\ \text{HABITAT} = \begin{bmatrix} \text{INTR} = [1] \begin{bmatrix} \text{SRC} = y_1 \in \mathcal{E} \\ \text{DEST} = y_2 \in \mathcal{E} \\ \text{TOP} = top(+Y) \\ \text{DIR} = align(Z, \mathcal{E}_{vec(y_2 - y_1)}) \end{bmatrix} \end{bmatrix} \\ \\ \text{AFFORD\_STR} = \begin{bmatrix} A_1 = H[1] \rightarrow [fly(x, y_1, y_2)] \mathcal{R}_{fly}(x) \end{bmatrix} \end{bmatrix}$$

The plane begins from a source heading to a destination. It must remain upright within the medium, and oriented along a trajectory from source to destination. These constraints allow the plane to fulfill its *telic* role "fly," encoded as an *affordance*, following (Gibson, 1977), and subject to various interpretations (e.g., Steedman (2002); Chao et al. (2015); Osiurak et al.(2017); Poddiakov (2018)).

Now consider the class of **agentive nominals**, such as *pilot*, *pianist*, and the agent from Figure 2b, *chainsaw operator*. All such nouns are typed with a TELIC value referring to a specific event, such as flying a plane, playing piano, or felling trees. Such latent event values are present by virtue of identifying the *typing* of the individual mentioned (in text) or portrayed (in an image).

Finally, consider the class of object **resultative nominals**, such as *debris* (Figure 3b), and the two examples shown below, i.e., *lava flow* and *laundry*.

Figure 4: Lava flow (left) and clean laundry (right)

As the name implies, the nominal makes reference to an event bringing about the denotation of the entity (Pustejovsky, 1995; Hovav and Levin, 2010). That is, *debris* is made of parts of a referenced, previously intact object, of which those constitutive parts still exist in some form, but no longer constitute the complete object. *Lava flow*, on the other hand, is actually a polysemous nominal, referring to either an event or the resulting material. Here, the image depicts the rock formation resulting from the event. Finally, the nominal *laundry* has a latent event referencing the resulting state of the clothes (either dirty or clean) being laundered. This image constrains the ambiguity to the clean state, as the folded clothes are situated over the dryer, two additional habitat constraints suggesting this interpretation. This is a signature example of a narrative constructed entirely from the composition of several objects and their associated latent event structures.

4 Future Directions

In this position paper, we argue that there is a potentially rich latent event structure associated with objects in text and images, which can be exploited for enriching the interpretation and construction of narratives. Objects can be seen as encoding latent event structures that, when combined, can create narrative structures of their own. This can potentially provide information for a framework within which to computationally extract linkages between images and text in news stories, and model coherent event sequences, and predict bias or differences of perspective in reporting. In order to test such hypotheses, we are currently annotating and analyzing a number of different corpora to identify both the TELIC roles and affordances associated with objects, as expressed in text and images. These include the Flikr30k (Young et al., 2014; Plummer et al., 2015); the VisualGenome (Krishna et al., 2017); and a subset of the images used for in the Visual Question Answering task from MS COCO (Lin et al., 2014). While there have been some efforts to identify affordances with objects (Chao et al., 2015), it remains a challenging issue to create object-latent event associations at scale. We believe a combination of manual annotation together with automatic extraction techniques for qualia relations (Cimiano and Wenderoth, 2007; Claveau and

Sébillot, 2013) will help in constructing a multimodal lexical resource that reflects the narrative structure of objects.

Acknowledgements

The authors would like to thank the reviewers for their helpful comments. We would also like Tuan Do, Kyeongmin Rim, Marc Verhagen, and David McDonald for discussion on the topic. This work is supported by a contract with the US Defense Advanced Research Projects Agency (DARPA), Contract CwC-W911NF-15-C-0238. Approved for Public Release, Distribution Unlimited. The views expressed are those of the authors and do not reflect the official policy or position of the Department of Defense or the U.S. Government.

References

Somak Aditya, Yezhou Yang, Chitta Baral, Cornelia Fermuller, and Yiannis Aloimonos. 2015. From images to sentences through scene description graphs using commonsense reasoning and knowledge. *arXiv preprint arXiv:1511.03292*.

Jacqueline Aguilar, Charley Beller, Paul McNamee, Benjamin Van Durme, Stephanie Strassel, Zhiyi Song, and Joe Ellis. 2014. A comparison of the events and relations across ace, ere, tac-kbp, and framenet annotation standards. In *Proceedings of the Second Workshop on EVENTS: Definition, Detection, Coreference, and Representation*, pages 45–53.

Peter Anderson, Basura Fernando, Mark Johnson, and Stephen Gould. 2016. Spice: Semantic propositional image caption evaluation. In *European Conference on Computer Vision*, pages 382–398. Springer.

Lamberto Ballan, Marco Bertini, Alberto Del Bimbo, Lorenzo Seidenari, and Giuseppe Serra. 2011. Event detection and recognition for semantic annotation of video. *Multimedia Tools and Applications*, 51(1):279–302.

Nathanael Chambers and Dan Jurafsky. 2009. Unsupervised learning of narrative schemas and their participants. In *Proceedings of the Joint Conference of the 47th Annual Meeting of the ACL and the 4th International Joint Conference on Natural Language Processing of the AFNLP: Volume 2-Volume 2*, pages 602–610. Association for Computational Linguistics.

Yu-Wei Chao, Zhan Wang, Rada Mihalcea, and Jia Deng. 2015. Mining semantic affordances of visual object categories. In *Computer Vision and Pattern Recognition (CVPR), 2015 IEEE Conference on*, pages 4259–4267. IEEE.

Philipp Cimiano and Johanna Wenderoth. 2007. Automatic acquisition of ranked qualia structures from the web. In *Proceedings of the 45th Annual Meeting of the Association of Computational Linguistics*, pages 888–895.

Vincent Claveau and Pascale Sébillot. 2013. Automatic acquisition of gl resources, using an explanatory, symbolic technique. In *Advances in Generative Lexicon Theory*, pages 431–454. Springer.

James J. Gibson. 1977. The theory of affordances. *Perceiving, Acting, and Knowing: Toward an ecological psychology*, pages 67–82.

S. Gupta and J. Malik. 2015. Visual Semantic Role Labeling. *ArXiv e-prints*, May.

Malka Rappaport Hovav and Beth Levin. 2010. Reflections on manner/result complementarity. In E. Doron, M. Rappaport Hovav, and I. Sichel, editors, *Syntax, Lexical Semantics, and Event Structure*, pages 21–38. Oxford University Press.

Ranjay Krishna, Yuke Zhu, Oliver Groth, Justin Johnson, Kenji Hata, Joshua Kravitz, Stephanie Chen, Yannis Kalantidis, Li-Jia Li, David A Shamma, et al. 2017. Visual genome: Connecting language and vision using crowdsourced dense image annotations. *International Journal of Computer Vision*, 123(1):32–73.

Nikhil Krishnaswamy and James Pustejovsky. 2016. Multimodal semantic simulations of linguistically underspecified motion events. In *Spatial Cognition X*, pages 177–197. Springer.

Tsung-Yi Lin, Michael Maire, Serge Belongie, James Hays, Pietro Perona, Deva Ramanan, Piotr Dollár, and C Lawrence Zitnick. 2014. Microsoft coco: Common objects in context. In *European conference on computer vision*, pages 740–755. Springer.

François Osiurak, Yves Rossetti, and Arnaud Badets. 2017. What is an affordance? 40 years later. *Neuroscience & Biobehavioral Reviews*, 77:403–417.

Bryan A Plummer, Liwei Wang, Chris M Cervantes, Juan C Caicedo, Julia Hockenmaier, and Svetlana Lazebnik. 2015. Flickr30k entities: Collecting region-to-phrase correspondences for richer image-to-sentence models. In *Proceedings of the IEEE international conference on computer vision*, pages 2641–2649.

Alexander N Poddiakov. 2018. Exploratory and counter-exploratory objects: Design of meta-affordances.

James Pustejovsky and Nikhil Krishnaswamy. 2016. VoxML: A visualization modeling language. In Nicoletta Calzolari (Conference Chair), Khalid Choukri, Thierry Declerck, Sara Goggi, Marko Grobelnik, Bente Maegaard, Joseph Mariani, Helene Mazo, Asuncion Moreno, Jan Odijk, and Stelios Piperidis, editors, *Proceedings of the Tenth International Conference on Language Resources and Evaluation (LREC 2016)*, Paris, France, May. European Language Resources Association (ELRA).

James Pustejovsky and Jessica Moszkowicz. 2011. The qualitative spatial dynamics of motion. *The Journal of Spatial Cognition and Computation*.

James Pustejovsky, José M Castano, Robert Ingria, Roser Sauri, Robert J Gaizauskas, Andrea Setzer, Graham Katz, and Dragomir R Radev. 2003. Timeml: Robust specification of event and temporal expressions in text. *New directions in question answering*, 3:28–34.

James Pustejovsky. 1995. *The Generative Lexicon*. MIT Press, Cambridge, MA.

James Pustejovsky. 2013a. Dynamic event structure and habitat theory. In *Proceedings of the 6th International Conference on Generative Approaches to the Lexicon (GL2013)*, pages 1–10. ACL.

James Pustejovsky. 2013b. Where things happen: On the semantics of event localization. In *Proceedings of ISA-9: International Workshop on Semantic Annotation*.

Marco Rospocher, Marieke van Erp, Piek Vossen, Antske Fokkens, Itziar Aldabe, German Rigau, Aitor Soroa, Thomas Ploeger, and Tessel Bogaard. 2016. Building event-centric knowledge graphs from news. *Web Semantics: Science, Services and Agents on the World Wide Web*, 37:132–151.

Mark Steedman. 2002. Plans, affordances, and combinatory grammar. *Linguistics and Philosophy*, 25(5-6):723–753.

Naushad UzZaman, Hector Llorens, Leon Derczynski, James Allen, Marc Verhagen, and James Pustejovsky. 2013. Semeval-2013 task 1: Tempeval-3: Evaluating time expressions, events, and temporal relations. In *Second Joint Conference on Lexical and Computational Semantics (* SEM), Volume 2: Proceedings of the Seventh International Workshop on Semantic Evaluation (SemEval 2013)*, volume 2, pages 1–9.

Mark Yatskar, Luke Zettlemoyer, and Ali Farhadi. 2016. Situation recognition: Visual semantic role labeling for image understanding. In *Proceedings of the IEEE Conference on Computer Vision and Pattern Recognition*, pages 5534–5542.

Peter Young, Alice Lai, Micah Hodosh, and Julia Hockenmaier. 2014. From image descriptions to visual denotations: New similarity metrics for semantic inference over event descriptions. *Transactions of the Association for Computational Linguistics*, 2:67–78.

A Rich Annotation Scheme for Mental Events

William Croft
Dept. of Linguistics
Univ. of New Mexico
wcroft@unm.edu

Pavlína Pešková
Dept. of Linguistics
Univ. of New Mexico
pavlinap@unm.edu

Michael Regan
Dept. of Linguistics
Univ. of New Mexico
reganman@unm.edu

Sook-kyung Lee
Dept. of Linguistics
Univ. of New Mexico
sklee@unm.edu

Abstract

We present a rich annotation scheme for the structure of mental events. Mental events are those in which the verb describes a mental state or process, usually oriented towards an external situation. While physical events have been described in detail and there are numerous studies of their semantic analysis and annotation, mental events are less thoroughly studied. The annotation scheme proposed here is based on decompositional analyses in the semantic and typological linguistic literature. The scheme was applied to the news corpus from the 2016 Events workshop, and error analysis of the test annotation provides suggestions for refinement and clarification of the annotation scheme.

1 Introduction

Many semantic annotation schemes have a very skeletal annotation of the event expressed by the verb in the clause: just the participants and the roles they play in the event. However, semantic role labels do not capture the details of the causal and other interactions between participants in events (Talmy, 1976; Talmy, 1985; Talmy, 1988), or the subevents that make up the event. For this reason, some have proposed a finer-grained annotation of events (Ikuta et al., 2014; Croft et al., 2016). These efforts have focused mainly on physical events: motion, change of (physical) state, force transmission, application/removal, creation/destruction and so on. This perhaps reflects the fact that the verbal semantics literature in theoretical linguistics has also focused mainly on physical events (Talmy, 1976; Talmy, 1988; Levin and Rappaport Hovav, 1995; Levin and Rappaport Hovav, 2005; Goldberg, 1995; Croft, 2012).

But much of what we talk about is about ourselves, including our mental states—perception, knowledge and belief and emotions—and how we interact with others. For example, in the news corpus used for the shared annotation task for the NAACL 2016 Workshop on Events, the corpus which we use for our test annotation, of the 779 main clause actual (real world, actually occurring) events, only 264 of them, or 34%, describe physical events. In the verbal semantics literature, there has been some attention to certain kinds of mental events (and hardly any attention to social events). However, there has not been a systematic attempt to analyze all types of mental events in the theoretical literature. The primary sources for the semantic analysis of mental events are therefore computational resources such as VerbNet (Kipper-Schuler, 2005; Palmer et al., 2017) and FrameNet (Baker et al., 1998; Ruppenhofer et al., 2016). While these resources are broad, the semantic analysis of FrameNet is restricted to participant roles (Frame Elements), though VerbNet has developed some predicate calculus representations to analyze event structure.

We propose an annotation scheme for different semantic types of mental events. The annotation scheme is intended to support a force dynamic decomposition of events that is at least partly attributable to the meanings of the argument structure constructions that mental verbs occur in. The force dynamic analysis is based on Talmy's (1976; 1988) analysis of event structure . In the force dynamic model, event structure is defined in terms of the interactions between the participants in the event. An argument structure construction is the configuration of subject, object and oblique phrases (governed by various

Proceedings of the Workshop on Events and Stories in the News, pages 7–17
Santa Fe, New Mexico, USA, August 20, 2018.

prepositions in English, sometimes expressed by case inflections in other languages) which a verb occurs with. Goldberg (1995; 2006) argues that an argument structure construction has a meaning which represents a highly schematic event structure.

It is this highly schematic event structure that we aim to annotate: it is schematic enough that a relatively small number of annotation categories can be used, but it provides more detailed information about the internal structure of events than semantic role labels on argument phrases. The mental event annotation scheme proposed here is compatible with the annotation scheme in the force dynamic representation proposed in Croft et al. (2016); however they analyze only physical events.

The argument for annotating the internal structure of events is twofold. First, many English verbs allow for different semantic interpretations when they occur in different argument structure constructions. The examples in (1) illustrate the ambiguity, with the standard labels for the force-dynamic type given in brackets:[1]

(1) a. She flailed with her feet to get her balance and managed to **kick** the chair. [contact]
     b. So he's going to shoot if I have to **kick** him black and blue. [change of state]
     c. **Kick** the ball into Lake Michigan... [ballistic motion]
     d. Go on, **kick** him the ball and let's see what he'll do with it. [transfer]
     e. You **kick** wildly at the plastic bottle, finally knocking it loose. [conative—action aimed towards a target entity]

Thus, a semantic annotation of the event expressed by a clause cannot rely simply on a verb's lexical semantics taken out of grammatical context.

Second, there is a strong correlation between a construction's form and the semantics of the event. That is, particular argument structure constructions have meaning, as Fillmore et al. (1988), Goldberg (1995; 2006) and other construction grammarians have argued. The correlation is not perfect: there is some lexical idiosyncrasy in the choice of prepositions for some argument structure constructions, for example. Also, some constructions are polysemous and have metaphorical uses, which means that their meaning is not completely determined by their form. Nevertheless, the need for semantic annotation of event structure partly independent of a verb's lexical semantics is evident from the many-to-many mapping between verbs and argument structure constructions.

Both of these arguments for the annotation of internal event structure apply to mental events, although to a lesser degree.

2   The Force Dynamic Structure of Mental Events

Mental verbs describe mental events, that is, mental states or processes of a person (or certain animals to whom internal mental states are attributed). These mental states or processes generally though not always occur oriented to some external situation: an entity, a static state of affairs, or the occurrence of a dynamic event. Mental events are usually divided into three domains: perception, cognition and emotion, with some linguists such as Levin (1993) and Verhoeven (2007) distinguishing desire/intention from emotion.

Mental events differ from physical events in two major ways. First, there is no physical transmission of force between the external situation and the person's mental state. Hence there is no force dynamic relation between participants. Nevertheless, mental events are construed as having "directionality". We will describe the varying construals of mental events as *mental force dynamics* or *mental dynamics* for short.

Second, what is happening in the mind is not outwardly apparent to the observer. Hence, the actual mental event—state or process, for example—is a construal by the observer who produces a sentence describing the mental event. Alternative construals of mental events are generally inferred from the grammatical constructions that mental predicates occur in, constructions that are often but not always used also for physical events. Tense-aspect constructions indicate whether the mental event is construed

---

[1] The examples in (1) are from Croft et al. (2016); they were taken from COCA and Google.

as a state or a process, and argument structure constructions indicate the "direction" of causation in mental events. In many cases, there is a lexical split between alternative construals of mental events.

Mental events have two primary participants, the person whose mental state/process is being described, usually called the *experiencer*, and the external situation (entity, etc.), called the *stimulus*; the stimulus of emotion predicates is also called the target/subject matter of emotion (T/SM) following Pesetsky (1995).

The semantics literature has described three common construals of the mental force dynamic relation between the experiencer and the stimulus. Viberg (1983), a cross-linguistic survey of the semantics of perception verbs, distinguishes *activity* from *experience* predicates, as illustrated in 2.[2]

(2)   a. Everyone was **looking** at you.

        b. I **see** garbage on people's side yards that they havent even picked up.

The activity construal corresponds to Levin's *Marvel* verb class 31.3 (Levin, 1993) (emotion verbs) and *Peer* verb class 30.3 (perception verbs; Levin does not include cognition verbs, which usually take sentential complements). The experience construal corresponds to Levin's *Admire* verb class 31.2 (emotion verbs) and *See* and *Sight* verb classes 30.1 and 30.2 (perception verbs).

In the third construal of the relationship that has been discussed in the literature, the external situation is construed as causing a mental state to occur in the experiencer (Zaenen, 1993; Pesetsky, 1995; Levin and Grafmiller, 2013; Doron, 2017).

(3)   a. But as much as they **annoyed** him, he annoyed them right back.

        b. But most of the exhibits will **surprise**, perhaps **startle**, and in some cases **delight** viewers.

In languages such as Hebrew (Doron, 2017) and Korean (example 4) there is explicit causative morphology in the causative construal.

(4) Senghankyung-i   tto   han-pen na-lul nolla-**ke**   **ha**-ess-ta
     Senhankyung-NOM again one-time I-ACC surprise-**CAU CAU**-PST-DECL
     'Senghankyung surprised me once again.' (Sejong Corpus)

The causative construal corresponds to Levin's *Amuse* verb class 31.1 (emotion verbs); there are no basic perception verbs with this construal.

Activity and experience perception events can be distinguished aspectually in English by the Progressive construction, which is sensitive to the stative-dynamic event distinction. English sometimes distinguishes activity and experience lexically (*look* vs. *see*). However, other verbs may have either construal:

(5)   a. You can **taste** the mixture to see if you want a stronger coffee flavor. [activity]

        b. I could almost **taste** a dish by watching it being prepared, especially if it was something simple. [experience]

This is an example of a single verb having alternative semantic interpretations that need to be distinguished, although in this case both construals use the same argument structure construction (the transitive).

Croft (1993) argues that there are consistent differences in argument structure across languages between the activity, causative and experience construals, and offers a "causal" analysis for the differences. The activity construal always expresses the experiencer as subject, and the stimulus as either object (as in Spanish *mirar*) or as an oblique, usually derived from a locative (as in English *look at*). The activity construal conceptualizes the mental event in terms of the experiencer directing her attention to the stimulus: the experiencer engages in a mental activity, usually volitionally, and hence is coded as subject.

The causative construal always expresses the stimulus as subject; the experiencer is expressed as object or as an oblique, typically dative. The causative construal conceptualizes the mental event in terms of the stimulus causing a mental state to occur in the experiencer, as described above; hence the stimulus as initiator of the event is subject.

---

[2]All examples in sections 2 and 3 are from the news segment of COCA unless otherwise indicated.

In contrast, the experience construal is variable: the experiencer may be subject or nonsubject, as in 6 (a nonsubject experiencer is often in a dative case, hence the term "dative experiencer"). Most English verbs have subject experiencers (Talmy, 1985). However, there are some English verbs taking the stimulus subject construction for the experience construal, namely Levin's *Appeal* verb class 31.4 (emotion) and her Stimulus Subject Perception Verb class 30.4 (perception).

(6)   a. We can now begin to **understand** the senseless act.

        b. What **appeals** to you might not **appeal** to your neighbor.

The experience construal conceptualizes both directing of attention by the experiencer and the change of mental state by the stimulus. Hence it is stative (no direction of causation), and either experiencer or stimulus may be expressed as subject.

There may be a subtle semantic difference in the experience construal when both argument structures are possible. When the experiencer is subject, they have greater control over the mental event, and when the experiencer is object, they have less control. In Yoruba, one of the major languages of Nigeria, the subject experiencer construction indicates that the experiencer has control over their anger, but the object experiencer construction indicates that the anger has come to them involuntarily (Rowlands, 1969).

(7)   **Mo** binú   *vs.* Inú bi   **mi**
        I   anger_inside   inside anger **me**
        'I am angry' *vs.* 'I feel/felt angry'

Pesetsky (1995) argues that some transitive constructions in English are ambiguous between what we are calling causative and experience construals. He argues that sentence 8 may mean that the article in the *Times* causes Bill to be angry at something else, for example corruption described in the article (the causative construal), or it may mean the same as sentence 9, namely that Bill has a mental state of anger with respect to the article, for example because it was written in a biased manner (the experience construal). Sentence 9 has only the experience construal.

(8)   The article in the *Times* **angered** Bill. (Pesetsky, 1995)

(9)   Bill **was angry** at the article in the *Times*. (Pesetsky, 1995)

Pesetsky observes that one cannot express both the causative of the mental state and the distinct situation towards which the caused mental state is directed in a simple clause in English, although a periphrastic causative construction can express both. However, Doron (2017) observes that it is possible to do so in Hebrew.

(10)   *The article in the *Times* **angered** Bill at the government.

(11)   The article in the *Times* **caused** Bill to **be angry** at the government. (Pesetsky, 1995)

(12)   ha-martse   **'inyen**   ota be-balshanut
        the lecturer **interested** her in-linguistics
        'The lecturer got her interested in linguistics.' (Doron, 2017)

A final issue is the occurrence of some emotion predicates in the progressive, such as *But she **isn't** rejoicing over her place in history.*. This does not seem to be the activity construal, since the activity construal requires some control over the mental state, and emotions generally cannot be controlled by the experiencer. It is possible that the progressive occurs here because the verb describes not just an emotional mental state but also outward action reflecting the mental state.

3   Towards an Annotation Scheme for Mental Events

Based on the analysis of mental events in the semantics literature summarized in section 2, we developed an annotation scheme for mental force dynamic relations. We applied this annotation scheme to the mental event verb classes in VerbNet. Specifically, we annotated each example sentence for each case frame for each verb class and subclass in VerbNet that describes mental events. The number of example sentences, and hence the number of VerbNet (sub)class case frames for mental events, is 233. In this process, we were obliged to add four additional annotations. Two of the four new annotations, Engage and Refrain, pertain to subevents functioning as arguments of the main clause predicate event, which is uncommon in physical events but frequent in mental events. The other two new annotations, Judge and Intend, represent mental dynamic construals beyond the three construals discussed in the semantics literature.

3.1   Attend and Affect

The core of the annotation consists of the three construals of mental force dynamics described in section 2. The activity construal represents an Attend relation between the experiencer and the stimulus (or T/SM). The experiencer directs her attention to the stimulus; this is generally a volitional activity on the part of the experiencer.

The causative construal represents an Affect relation between the experiencer and the stimulus. The stimulus, which as noted above may be an entity, a state of affairs, or an occurrence of a dynamic event, brings about a mental state in the experiencer. This is not physical causation, let alone volitional causation, but what Talmy (1976) calls affective causation. Affect is also the force dynamic relation between an event of any kind and a Beneficiary (or "Maleficiary") who is positively (or adversely) affected by the event, as in *A school bookkeeper baked a cake **for Gurley** with purple-and-gold icing, the school colors.* In this case, as in (2016), a single clause will be annotated for two segments of the causal chain, the "core" event and the participant in the Affect relation with respect to the core event.

3.2   Experience and Experience*

The experience construal represents both Attend and Affect at once (see section 2), that is, one "direction" of causation is not highlighted at the expense of the other; as a result, the relation is construed as stative. However, for annotation purposes, we represent the double construal simply as a distinct, third type of construal, an Experience relation between experiencer and stimulus. This construal is generally a stative relation holding between the two participants, as in examples 13 and 15. It can also have an inceptive aspectual construal, as in examples 14 and 16; an inceptive construal is not uncommon among normally stative predicates.

(13)   I **see** garbage on peoples side yards that they havent even picked up.

(14)   Stead walked out the back door and suddenly **saw** a bobcat holding in its jaws a dead rabbit

(15)   But I don't really **remember** much about the clock.

(16)   I started to cross-examine them but suddenly **remembered** I'd left the tire iron inside the house.

We also distinguish between the experiential construal in which the experiencer is subject (Experience) and the construal in which the stimulus is subject (Experience*). The purpose of distinguishing these alternative argument linkings is to allow for the mapping of the referents of the subject and object phrases to the correct semantic participant roles. Also, in those languages that distinguish alternative construals semantically, as in the Yoruba sentences given in example 7, Experience and Experience* allows us to capture the distinct semantic interpretations of the alternative construals.

3.3   Engage and Refrain

The stimulus for a mental event need not be an entity but may be a state of affairs or the fact of an event occurring. In some cases, the state of affairs is expressed as an event nominal, as in example 17 below. In this case, the Experience relation holds between the experiencer and a stimulus that represents a state of affairs. In another case, the state of affairs is expressed as a sentential complement, particularly with cognitive verbs (propositional attitude verbs), as in example 18. These are analyzed in force dynamic terms in the same way as example 17. (For now, we are not distinguishing between propositions and events as complement types.)

(17)   I could understand **[their action]**.

(18)   She then discovered **[that a purse was missing]**.

In yet other cases, the state of affairs is divided syntactically between the "subject" and the "predicate" of the state of affairs, as in example 19. The noun phrase *a threat* is traditionally described as a predicative complement. In order to simplify the mapping between the syntactic structure and the semantic structure, we treat the state of affairs' "subject" and "predicate" as two separate "arguments", and posit an Engage relation between the two (that is, the referent of *it* Engages in the property of being a threat). In fact, there are only two event participants, the experiencer and the stimulus state of affairs, namely that it is a threat.

(19)   But in a June 2005 survey, by a 48% to 44% margin, more respondents judged **[it] [a threat]**.

We have also tentatively posited the negative counterpart to Engage, Refrain, since the syntactic construction for Refrain in English differs from the construction for Engage (*Rebuilding a life in Black Forest won't completely free **[her] [of the emotional turmoil that has marked the past year]**, she said.*); as noted above, one of the goals of this annotation scheme is to capture the semantics of the argument structure constructions that mental event verbs occur in.

3.4   Judge

In addition, we posited another distinct mental dynamic image scheme, Judge. Judge describes an active mental process mostly under the control of the experiencer, like Attend: it describes mental processes such as comparing, categorizing, inferring and measuring something. Unlike Attend, however, Judge describes the result of the mental process: the conclusion, classification or measurement arrived at. The result is often expressed as a predicative complement, as in example 19.

3.5   Intend

The final mental dynamic image schema that we added to our annotation is Intend, for the relationship between a volitional agent and the agent's as yet unrealized, and possibly never realized, action with respect to the other participant. The Intend relation can be used for an intended subevent of a physical action. For example, in *This is the way to cook a chicken for any kind of cold chicken salad, Asian or Western*, the agent performs a physical action on the chicken, but there is an intended subsequent subevent of preparing a cold chicken salad which is not (yet) realized in this sentence. Hence the Intend relation can be used for purpose arguments for all types of events, not unlike Affect with respect to the beneficiary of an event..

There are other verbs in which there are only two participants, the agent and the entity towards which the agent's intention is directed. These include verbs of searching, caring and longing.

(20)   Police were **searching** for a man suspected in the shooting.

(21)   She **cared** for her grandchild until the end.

(22)   She **looked** after him for years in the orphanage after their birth mother died.

(23)   They seem to **long** for the "good old days" that are forever gone.

(24)   What outdoor cook doesn't **lust** after one of those giant stainless steel grills, a mini-fridge and a sink with hot and cold running water?

Searching verbs and caring verbs do involve physical actions on the part of the agent, but the action is directed towards a potentially unrealized subevent pertaining to the endpoint of the causal chain: finding what is being searched for, and continued good condition of what is being cared for. Verbs of longing, on the other hand, are more purely mental events. However, all three verb classes use the construction [Subject Verb *for/after* Oblique], with the prepositions *for/after* that are characteristic of the intention/purpose construction. For this reason, we have included all of these categories in our annotation of mental events.

Intend cannot be reduced to Attend, although both describe the directing of some sort of mental state towards an external stimulus that is not (yet) affected. Example 25 is an Attend relation, using a locative

Annotation	Brief definition (Exp = experiencer, Stm = stimulus)
Attend	Exp directs attention to Stm: dynamic, volitional, no change to Stm.
Affect	Stm causes change of mental state of Exp: dynamic, causative. Used also to describe a Beneficiary/Maleficiary subevent in other types of events.
Experience	A perceptual, cognitive or emotional relation holds between Exp and Stm: stative (or inceptive), Exp is grammatical subject.
Experience*	A perceptual, cognitive or emotional relation holds between Exp and Stm: stative (or inceptive), Stm is grammatical subject.
Judge	Exp discerns or confers a perceptual, conceptual or evaluative status on an entity or a relation between entities: dynamic, volitional, no change to Stm.
Intend	Agent intends to act on another participant in some way but action on the participant is not realized: no change (yet) to participant. Used also to describe a Purpose subevent in other types of events.
Engage	A relation between an argument denoting a participant and another argument denoting the event/subevent that the participant is involved with. The participant is a core participant in the event.
Refrain	A relation between an argument denoting a participant and another argument denoting an event/subevent that the participant ends up *not* being involved with. The participant is a core participant in the event.

Table 1: Annotation scheme for mental events

preposition for the auditory stimulus that attention is being directed to; but example 26 describes a mental activity directed towards a specific sound which may or may not ever be heard by the experiencer.

(25) I **listened to** the record again (recently) for the first time in years.

(26) I **listened for** any sound of life and screamed for help.

As noted above, some semanticists distinguish verbs of desire from other emotion verbs. Levin (1993) distinguishes two subclasses of desire verbs, *Want* verbs and *Long* verbs. Unlike *Want* verbs, *Long* verbs express their "stimulus" with *for/after* in English, like other verbs of intention. For this reason, we have analyzed verbs of longing as instances of the Intend mental dynamic relation. Since *Want* verbs are semantically very similar, one might consider whether they are also instances of Intend. However, *Long* verbs may also construe the mental event as dynamic, similar to verbs of searching or caring, whereas *Want* verbs are stative.

(27) Dorothy **needs /*is needing** new shoes. (Levin, 1993)

(28) Dana **longs/is longing** for a sunny day. (Levin, 1993)

We therefore conclude based on both syntactic and semantic differences that *Want* verbs represent an Experience construal of the desire event, while *Long* verbs represent an Intend construal.

4 Applying the Annotation Scheme to Mental Events

The annotation scheme for mental events is summarized in Table 1. The scheme was tested by having two annotators involved in our project annotate the mental events in the news corpus used for the 2016 Events Workshop shared task. This news corpus contains a total of 3749 events annotated in Richer Event Description (RED) annotation, which does not annotate for force dynamics. We restricted our annotation to actual real-world events: we excluded nonfinite forms, including nominals, adjectives and prepositions, examining only primary predications. We also excluded coreferring events, some of which overlap with the previous categories. This filtering was done to avoid issues with annotating aspect and unrealized events, also part of this project although not the topic of this paper.

The filtering process left 779 events. We have no reason to believe that the distribution and type of events in the excluded categories are different from the distribution and type of events (physical, mental, social) included in our analysis. In other words, we believe that the force dynamic classification of events in the sample of 779 events is representative of the 3749 events in the total corpus. We used the VerbNet verb classification for an initial filter for mental events, and then hand-filtered the result. This left 156 mental events, of which a further 43 were deemed not to be mental events in the course of the annotation exercise. In other words, mental events make up around 15% of the 779 events in the news corpus. This is a relatively small number, but we expect that some of the mental dynamic analysis will carry over to the social events—which make up 51% of the 779 events—since social interaction involves persons using their mental faculties in the interaction. It is also possible that conversational data, where people frequently talk about other people including their beliefs and attitudes, will have a greater proportion of mental events compared to news stories.

A trial annotation of 25 sentences was performed by the two annotators and discussed by the annotators, the adjudicator and two other participants in the project. This led to clarification of the informal guidelines for the application of the annotation scheme, and the exclusion of 4 examples which were determined not to be mental events. The test annotation was then done on 92 remaining sentences; a further 39 sentences were excluded before the text annotation as not mental events (see section 5). The test annotation consisted of 92 tokens; there was 81% agreement in annotation (75 out of 92), with a Cohen's kappa of .85. As usual, it is difficult to compare the scoring of our semantic annotation to other semantic annotation tasks. Our force dynamic analysis annotates the combination of verb semantic class and the argument structure construction and the meaning it contributes, so that task itself is also not easily comparable to other verbal semantic annotation tasks.

5   Error Analysis

The analysis of inter-annotator disagreements in the test annotation indicated a number of areas in which the annotation scheme can be improved.[3]

A content issue that arose in the test annotation is distinguishing cognition from communication events with an unexpressed addressee. Cognition and communication share much conceptual structure: both describe propositional attitudes, both can alternatively construe the propositional content as a topic (Boas, 2010), and both have a cognizer of the content/topic.

Communication events of course also have a second cognizer, the addressee. But it is sometimes rather subtle to decide whether the verb without an addressee entails that the propositional content must be expressed verbally and hence must describe a communication event. For example, support of a political position, as in *Skelton was a social conservative who **supported** gun rights*, is frequently verbalized, since politicians are expected to express their political views; but it was concluded that a person can support (believe in) a particular policy without necessarily expressing it to anyone, and hence *support* can describe a mental event.

On the other hand, the negative evaluation of *condemn* in *Michaloliakos **condemned** the murder last month of a 34-year-old hip-hop artist and anti-fascist, Pavlos Fyssas, by a self-professed supporter of Golden Dawn* is necessarily a speech act and hence is a communication event. 22 examples were reclassified as communication events, and the guidelines have been clarified to specify whether or not verbal expression of the mental state is inherently part of the verb meaning.

Some emotional states can emerge without there being a clear external situation that brings it about, as in *But I **feel** so good....* We concluded that we had to posit a distinct annotation category, State, to represent an autonomous mental state that is not presented as part of a mental force dynamic relation to an external situation. The State mental event type is not found in VerbNet, possibly due to the fact that syntactically *good* is an adjective, not a verb.

A second issue is the fact that the same verb may have different mental force dynamic construals. This is of course the primary reason for positing such construals as part of constructional meaning. In some cases, the difference is indicated by a difference in the tense-aspect construction rather than the argument structure construction.

(29)   [The British Foreign Office] **was considering** his request for a meeting with Hague.

(30)   According to the Arizona Republic, Kyrsten Sinema **is thinking** of running.

(31)   A saffron red thread called a tilak, worn around the wrist **is considered** to have deep religious significance among Hindus,

---

[3]All examples in this section are from the 2016 NAACL Events Workshop shared task news corpus.

(32) I **thought** the point of an ecumenical council was to clarify essentialy (*sic*) there is a despute
      (*sic*) over the right faith and the council "decide" what is.

Examples 29 and 30 construe the mental event as dynamic and hence they describe the experiencer
directing their cognitive attention towards the event, that is, the Attend relation. In contrast, examples
31 and 32 are stative and hence they describe the Experience relation holding between the experiencer
and the stimulus situation. In addition, the latter two also express the situation as a finite complement
clause, the typical expression of the propositional content of the cognitive experience. In contrast, 29 and
30 use event nominals to express the state of affairs being considered. Although the argument structure
constructions are sometimes idiosyncratic in what mental dynamic relation they encode, the occurrence
of the Progressive is a reliable cue that the mental dynamic relation is Attend as opposed to Experience.

A third issue that arose in the test annotation pertains to the difference between adjectival passives–an
adjective with a passive participle form–and verbal passives (Wasow, 1977). A verb like *annoy* is usually
construed as a causative, and the passive with *by* for the stimulus/causing participant is simply the passive
voice version of the causative (Affect) construal. However, there also exists an adjectival form which is
identical to the passive participle, but governs the stimulus with a lexically idiosyncratic preposition,
one of the metaphorical locative prepositions typically found with the stimulus of mental events. The
adjectival form is an instance of the Experience construal.

(33) He was **annoyed by** her hectoring. (COCA News corpus) [Affect]

(34) I was **annoyed at** him, for interfering in the elections, giving statements here and there. (COCA
      News corpus) [Experience]

Wasow (1977) observes that the adjectival and verbal passive forms are mostly easily distinguished
in their syntactic behavior, with one exception: *known*; but *known* with a predicative complement, such
as example 35, is the verbal passive (cf. the active counterpart *They know him as/to be an expert on
national defense*). Example 35 and two other examples of *be known* in the test annotation were labeled
Experience instead of (passive) Affect.

(35) Skelton, who was first elected to the House in 1976, **was known as** an expert on national defense

6   Conclusion

Mental events have not been studied in detail in approaches to a finer-grained annotation of events. The
verbal semantics literature in theoretical linguistics has identified three common construals of events,
which we have annotated as Attend, Affect and Experience (including Experience* for the alternative
linking of the stimulus to the subject grammatical role). However, we needed to add two other mental
dynamic construals, Intend and Judge, plus two construals, Engage and Refrain, for subevents.

The text annotation provided fairly reliable interannotator agreement. Error analysis indicated a number of subtle annotation judgements that can be honed with more explicit guidelines to distinguish cognition from communication events when the latter have an unexpressed addressee, adjectival passives from
verbal passives, and to exploit aspectual as well as argument structure cues in the syntactic constructions.
In sum, however, the task of annotating VerbNet mental event classes and annotating news corpora has
led to a relatively stable annotation scheme for mental event structure.

Acknowledgements

This research was partly funded by grant number HDTRA1-15-0063 from the Defense Threat Reduction
Agency to the first author.

References

Collin F. Baker, Charles J. Fillmore, and John B. Lower. 1998. The Berkeley FrameNet project. In *Proceedings of COLING/ACL*, pages 86–90. Association for Computational Linguistics.

Hans Boas. 2010. The syntax-lexicon continuum in Construction Grammar: a case study of English communication verbs. *Belgian Journal of Linguistics*, 24:54–82.

William Croft, Pavlína Pešková, and Michael Regan. 2016. Annotation of causal and aspectual structure of events in RED: a preliminary report. In *4th Events Workshop, 15th Annual Conference of the North American Chapter of the Association of Computational Linguistics: Human Language Technologies*, NAAACL-HLT 2016, pages 8–17. Stroudsburg, Penn: Association for Computational Linguistics.

William Croft. 1993. Case marking and the semantics of mental verbs. In James Pustejovsky, editor, *Semantics and the Lexicon*, pages 55–72. Dordrecht: Kluwer Academic.

William Croft. 2012. *Verbs: aspect and causal structure*. Oxford: Oxford University Press.

Edith Doron. 2017. The causative component of locative and psychological verbs. Paper presented at the Workshop on Linguistic Perspectives on Causation, The Hebrew University of Jerusalem.

Charles J. Fillmore, Paul Kay, and Mary Catherine O'Conner. 1988. Regularity and idiomaticity in grammatical constructions: The case of let alone. *Language*, 64:501–538.

Adele E. Goldberg. 1995. *Constructions: A Construction Grammar Approach to Argument Structure*. Chicago: University of Chicago Pres.

Adele E. Goldberg. 2006. *Constructions at work: the nature of generalization in language*. Oxford: Oxford University Press.

Rei Ikuta, William F. Styler, Mariah Hamang, Tim O'Gorman, and Martha Palmer. 2014. Challenges of adding causation to richer event descriptions. In *Proceedings of the 2nd Workshop on EVENTS: Definition, Detection, Conference, and Representation*, pages 12–20. Association for Computational Linguistics.

Karin Kipper-Schuler. 2005. *VerbNet: A broad-coverage, comprehensive verb lexicon*. Ph.D. thesis, University of Pennsylvania.

Beth Levin and Jason Grafmiller. 2013. Do you always fear what frightens you? In Tracy Holloway King and Valeria de Paiva, editors, *From Quirky Case to Representing Space*, pages 21–32. CSLI Publications.

Beth Levin and Malka Rappaport Hovav. 1995. *Unaccusativity: at the syntax-lexical semantics interface*. Cambridge, Mass: MIT Press.

Beth Levin and Malka Rappaport Hovav. 2005. *Argument realization*. Cambridge: Cambridge University Press.

Beth Levin. 1993. *English verb classes and alternations: a preliminary investigation*. Chicago: University of Chicago Press.

Martha Palmer, Claire Bonial, and Jena D Hwang. 2017. VerbNet: Capturing English verb behavior, meaning and usage. In Susan Chipman, editor, *The Oxford Handbook of Cognitive Science*, pages 315–336. Oxford: Oxford University Press.

David Pesetsky. 1995. *Zero Syntax: Experiencers and Cascades*. Cambridge, Mass: MIT Press.

Evan Colyn Rowlands. 1969. *Yoruba*. Sevenoaks, Kent: Hodder and Stoughton.

Josef Ruppenhofer, Michael Ellsworth, Miria R. L. Petruck, Christopher R. Johnson, Collin F. Baker, and Jan Scheffczyk. 2016. *FrameNet II: Extended Theory and Practice*. Available at `https://framenet.icsi.berkeley.edu/fndrupal/the_book`.

Leonard Talmy. 1976. Semantic causative types. In Masayoshi Shibatani, editor, *The grammar of causative constructions*, volume 6, pages 43–116. New York: Academic Press.

Leonard Talmy. 1985. Lexicalization patterns: semantic structure in lexical forms. In Timothy Shopen, editor, *Language typology and syntactic description: grammatical categories and the lexicon*, volume 3, pages 57–149. Cambridge: Cambridge University Press.

Leonard Talmy. 1988. Force dynamics in language and cognition. *Cognitive Science*, 2:49–100.

Elisabeth Verhoeven. 2007. *Experiential Constructions in Yucatec Maya: a typologically based analysis of a function domain in a Mayan language*. John Benjamins Publishing Company.

Ake Viberg. 1983. The verbs of perception: a typological study. *Linguistics*, 21(1):123–162.

Thomas Wasow. 1977. Transformations and the lexicon. In Peter W. Culicover et al., editor, *Formal Syntax*, pages 327–360. New York: Academic Press.

Annie Zaenen. 1993. Unaccusativity in Dutch: Integrating syntax and lexical semantics. In James Pustejovsky, editor, *Semantics and the lexicon*, pages 129–61. Dordrecht: Kluwer Academic.

Cross-Document Narrative Alignment of Environmental News: A Position Paper on the Challenge of Using Event Chains to Proxy Narrative Features

Ben Miller

Emory University

b.j.miller@emory.edu

Abstract

Cross-document event chain co-referencing in corpora of news articles would achieve increased precision and generalizability from a method that consistently recognizes narrative, discursive, and phenomenological features such as tense, mood, tone, canonicity and breach, person, hermeneutic composability, speed, and time. Current models that capture primarily linguistic data such as entities, times, and relations or causal relationships may only incidentally capture narrative framing features of events. That limits efforts at narrative and event chain segmentation, among other predicate tasks for narrative search and narrative-based reasoning. It further limits research on audience engagement with journalism about complex subjects. This position paper explores the above proposition with respect to narrative theory and ongoing research on segmenting event chains into narrative units. Our own work in progress approaches this task using event segmentation, word embeddings, and variable length pattern matching in a corpus of 2,000 articles describing environmental events. Our position is that narrative features may or may not be implicitly captured by current methods explicitly focused on events as linguistic phenomena, that they are not explicitly captured, and that further research is required.

1   Introduction

A story is not so much a unique container to be read in isolation, but a locus of potential and actual connections to other stories and their representations. Those connections enable, among other things, critical inference and empathic reading, or the sharing of a feeling from a story based on successfully imagining a character's perspective. News literacy (Fleming 2014, Hornik 2017), as taught at the Stony Brook Center for News Literacy, the Berkman Center, and the Rockefeller, Revson, McCormick, and Knight Foundations backed News Literacy Project center on teaching how to think critically about news, a skill similarly predicated on one's ability to evaluate and connect narratives. Understanding the narrative framing used to convey specific topics in journalism, such as news about the environment, may help explain aspects of audience engagement and comprehension.

Technologies like RDF and XML allow for the hardcoding of some of those connections in to a document at its moment of composition, but most stories, even those published by contemporary news organizations, lack the rigorous indexing they make possible. RDF, rather than directing semantic annotation at the moment of composition, is a model that can guide annotation projects taking place after publication (Vossen and Cybulska 2017). And while advancements in unifying annotations like Richer Event Description (O'Gorman et al. 2016) and schema based approaches (Simonson and Davis 2016) can increase the aggregation of existing automated annotation strategies or advance work to elucidate narrative schemas via document categorization, neither model explicitly addresses what narratologists like Genette (1980), Bal (1985), Ryan (1991), Bruner (1991), or Mani (2014) have identified as core attributes of narrative. Without explicitly capturing those core attributes, and without evaluating the extent to which those attributes are indirectly captured, tasks like critical reading, inference, and em-

Proceedings of the Workshop on Events and Stories in the News, pages 18–24
Santa Fe, New Mexico, USA, August 20, 2018.

pathic reading cannot be modeled successfully as they depend on discursive and phenomenological aspects of perspective like tempo, mood, person, tense, intentional state entailment, hermeneutic composability, and tone.

Capturing these features of narrative technique, such as the varying differential in speed between the passage of time between all the events in a chain that could have been documented (story time) and the passage of time between the events in a chain that were documented (narrative time), would, I contend, further research on the conceptual, emotional, and persuasive nature of narrative. However, that work first necessitates documenting the granular, connective tissue of narrative.

One domain in journalism that could benefit from increased sensitivity to narratological features is reporting on the environment. In the American context, a significant impediment to pro-environmental policy seem to be the opinions of the general public. Those opinions are shaped by social forces, including reportage on the environment. Identifying and demonstrating the narratological features used to frame different environmental stories such as weather and climatic events may help reveal connections among different populations and their stance towards environmental policy. A narrative, in the context of news about the environment, could be defined variously depending upon the particular question motivating the study. In regards to this study, it is comprised of events organized and related in such a way so as to allow for the recognition of features described by the above list of narratologists.

2   Blending Linguistic and Conceptual Descriptions of Narrative

The granular form these cross-document connections take, as identified by computational linguistics, are linguistic phenomena such as exophora, entity mentions when an entity is known in advance to be notable, absolute references such as to locations or measurements, and bibliographic citations. Exophora are the anaphoric, pronominal references that stretch across texts. This already high bar for meaningful cross-document annotations is even more challenging than it appears because, as with conceptual metaphors, these linguistic tokens are indicators of a phenomena, rather than the phenomena itself. The current shorthand is to identify a token that expresses an event (Ponti and Korhonen 2017), then annotate that token or set of tokens (Simonson 2016). For what we have described as concrete events in relation to human rights violations (e.g. events that have a particular physical outcome that is relatively independent of interpretation, such as an unlawful killing), the conflation of the linguistic and the conceptual is not highly problematic, as even simple string-based information retrieval of that type of information accounted for an F_1 score of 0.80 (Miller et al. 2014). Moving beyond this kind of superficial engagement to more conceptual categories of event knowledge is a task not dissimilar to engaging with conceptual metaphors.

Problematically for computational linguistics, even in projects reliant on manual annotation, interannotator agreement for rich metaphor annotation is relatively low when compared to annotation of other linguistic features such as entity category. Gordon (2015) found pairwise Cohen κ scores of 0.65 and 0.42 for annotations of 14 categories of conceptual metaphors in 1,450 sentences across their three annotators. In regard to narrative annotation, Finlayson (2015) returned a strict F1-score of 0.22 and a generous F1-score of 0.71 for interannotator agreement on manual labeling of Proppian functions. Implementing annotation for the full taxonomy for Genette's narrative schema (1983), an as yet unattempted task, would require annotations for four levels of distance, four narrator functions, four type of time, five levels, four speeds, three orders, and three frequencies. The results of Gordon et al.'s work, and the complexity of narratological frameworks indicates that there is a great deal of distance between the linguistic token and the conceptual framing described by narrative theory.

The misleading slippage between the notion of a token as an indicator and a token as the phenomena to be indicated is common in the literature on language processing of conceptual phenomena. For example, in the guidelines defining an event for the Automatic Content Extraction (ACE) program, the Linguistic Data Consortium states the following: "An Event is a specific occurrence involving participants. An Event is something that happens. An Event can frequently be described as a change of state. We will not be tagging all Events, but only examples of a particular set of types and subtypes" (LDC 2005). What is valuable at this point is not the particular definition of an event put forward by ACE, one oddly compliant with the Russian Formalist definition of an event from 1925 (Shklovsky 1991), but the conflation of event with the particular text that will be tagged. The TERQAS workshop productively complicated the definition of events as stative or dynamic situations occurring within a particular focal extent (Pustejovsky et al. 2003). This definition blends the linguistic understanding necessary to develop a computational approach with a narratological approach sensitive to focalization and storytelling. Contemporary representations of these definitions, such as that developed as the Event and Situation Ontology (Segers et al. 2015), focus on linking dynamic and stative events in conceptual frames so as to enable better inferencing. The last complication we will address and one core to our work, as described in Sprungnoli and Tonelli (2016), is that each domain, e.g. history, journalism, literary studies, most likely has many competing, useful, underspecified definitions of what constitutes an event, and that those definitions have functions not addressed by an event definition driven by what is computationally tractable. Those domains address critical questions of influence, veridicality, and resonance that may require rethinking how to bridge the ontological and the linguistic.

3   Narrative structure as critical reading

Given the power of event chains as conceptual containers to further critical reading strategies like inferencing, our work aims at the cross-document coreference of meaningful chains while preserving their ontological and conceptual, rather than their linguistic instantiations.

Existing methods in similar work by Simonson and Davis (2015), Chambers and Jurafsky (2009), Bean and Rilof (2004), and Bagga and Baldwin (1999), focused in an incremental way on how to build approximations of narrative structures that included actors in various roles. For an example of how investigations into narrative schemas can facilitate critical thinking, Simonson and Davis (2015) raises the question as to why event chains extracted from articles indexed by the New York Times which were otherwise classified as "Murders and Attempted Murders," were not, when police officers were the ones performing the shootings and killings. Aspects of each story's focalization in relation to the schemas that incorporate those aspects, might facilitate better understanding as to why that disconnect is true. Bruner (1991) supports this reading in his exploration of canonicity and the breach; a narrative must draw on two competing pre-existing cultural tropes, a script that sets the background expectations and a breach which violates that script in ways that are often expected, but still worth telling. Retelling a visit to a restaurant evokes a canonical script but, per Bruner, is not a narrative. When the tip is a winning lottery ticket, the owner a long-lost relative, or the server spills a beverage to some later consequence, that script is breached in an expected, but interesting way.

One way in which those methods fall short of the ambitious goal of automatically capturing narrative strategies is that what they explicitly capture is not narrative, but events, semantic roles, dependencies, verbs, nouns, and scripts. Adoption of schema performance measures such as the narrative Cloze test (Chamers and Jurafsky 2008), demonstrate this, as the Cloze test effectively measures canonicity, but not breach, and is therefore more suited for measuring the accuracy of scripts than of narratives. While those methods may also indirectly capture narrative features, it is unclear at this point whether any of them do, and if so, to what extent. These limits contradict the central role posited by cognitive theories of narrative from Lewis (1978) and Johnson-Laird (1983) to Bruner (1991) and Gervas (2016). Narrative, for those theorists, functions as a means of organizing and communicating information about the world from the perspective of the narrator. As such, narrative offers a vehicle with which embedded knowledge of an environment is simultaneously interpreted and captured, then disseminated in a highly complex structure. Integrating Bruner's 10-point schema of narrative diachronicity, particularity, intentional state entailment, hermeneutic composability, canonicity and breach, referentiality, genericness, normativeness, context sensitivity and negotiability, and narrative accrual with Genette's would offer an ontology blending phenomenological approach and discursive approaches. In essence, it would allow for aligning event chains across documents in regard to their linguistic, phenomenological, and discursive perspectives, allowing for narrative alignment to recognize correspondences across both event as documentation of a phenomena, and event as documentation of a complex perspective.

Given the challenge of recognizing meaningful—e.g., multivariate—connections between documents, our work begins with a series of simplifying assumptions. First is that events and narrative features have meanings that are stable after they are extracted from a particular story and stored in a new format. Second, an event can be indicated by a continuous or discontinuous linguistic token or set of tokens such that while annotation is required, paraphrasing and glossing are not. Third, that a particular linguistic token that stands in for an event is commensurate with semantically similar tokens in other contexts and documents. And lastly, that the general applicability of a priori morphological frameworks like Propp's

(1968) functions is limited despite expansions and emendations (Gilet, 1998; Gervas 2013; Finlayson 2016). Applications of Propp's framework beyond his primary corpus of Russian fairy tales from the Afanasyev collection have required extensive adjustments. Dundes (1963), in his analysis of Native American folk tales, used a similar morphological approach focused on motifemes that blended the work of Propp, Kenneth Pike, and Stith Thompson. To connect with Propp's framework, he equated the disequilibrium-to-equilibrium transition common to his corpus to be equivalent to either a state of either surplus or lack. Dundes did so, as the second state, lack, motivated the stories Propp analysed. Those using Propp's functions note that his work was intended to support a multicultural analysis of folklore, but that the schema is limited in its descriptive power. Colby (1973) in his discussion of North Alaskan Eskimo folktales has to alter Propp's morphological framework to suit a different cultural tradition. Though functions are still defined by their position in a narrative sequence, he introduces two other mechanisms that define a function: sequence structures such as loops, and categorical rules operative when figures appear in certain sets. These new components of narrative he named Eidons, indicating that only five of Propp's 31 functions were relevant for his corpus. Studies like these demonstrate the extensive theoretical work necessary to generalize morphological approaches for narrative analysis. Not only were new functions necessary, but the story grammar itself, the basis of a morphological approach alongside the notion of a narrative's divisibility, required new rules.

These descriptive boundaries for schemas like Propp's show that this type of structural approach is an example of a phenomenological-discursive framework; Propp, Dundes, and Colby each described narrative with a technical structure from a limited perspective and that description is most valuable for understanding the world represented by their respective corpora.

4 Examples of narrative structure in stories about the weather

This study's preliminary empirical work began by finding concrete events using token-focused methods from four corpora drawn from contemporary news articles about the environment. The four corpora themselves each comprised 532-584 articles from 2000-2010 drawn from English-language publications with each article ranging in length from 750-1250 words. The total corpus is 2,258 articles spanning 1.96m tokens. Respectively, the corpora on earthquakes, hurricanes, pollution, and tsunami referenced terms associated with deaths or injuries 875, 334, 208, and 681 times, respectively. The references described events as varied as, "killed more than 230,000 people," and "killed 35,322 people in Sri Lanka," in an article about an earthquake and one about a tsunami, to "left at least 200 people dead or missing" in a report about a hurricane, to "oxygen starved dead zones," in an article about pollution. While inferences can be drawn about the way each of those events are covered and the human cost of natural and man-made disasters, assessing the deployment of more ontological categories of narrative understanding such as canonicity and breach to each of these fatal events is what would enable more complex, critical engagement.

As an example, consider the phrase, "dead or missing." This nomenclature only appears 21 times across the 2,258 articles about natural disasters. Of those 21 times, 14 are in articles about tsunami, 1 in an article about a hurricane, and 6 in articles about earthquakes (of which one was about the combined earthquake-tsunami event that devastated Fukushima, Japan). In one article on the 2004 Indian Ocean tsunami, the narrative unit centered on the stative event, "dead or missing," proceeds as follows. A local official is quoted as recounting that victims' bodies have been identified, but his knowledge is put forward as lacking in relation to the national origin of those individuals. One country is put forward as particularly hard-hit with an explanation provided for why, and an official from the foreign country is quoted enumerating the toll, indicating the method of identification, and suggesting that the work of identification and repatriation will be more difficult from here on. Comparing the elements of this article's narrative versus the narrative elements of other articles describing similar events has the potential to reveal, for example, both aspects of canonicity and breach, and issues of what Bruner calls hermeneutic composability. That term refers to the range of possible interpretations supported by a given set of phrases, a range that journalism, and computational approaches suggest we limit by selecting the most common interpretation. Aligning narratives about similar events within a corpus would allow for the evaluation of that process, one Bruner refers to as narrative banalization. While not a feature of a narrative per se, evaluating the relationships between narratives and the events they purport to convey is a core task for the computational analyses of narrative.

5   Conclusions and future work

Based on work like Simonson (2018), Caselli and Vossen (2017), and Spurgnoli and Tonelli (2016) that focus on linguistic event chain extraction, and work like that reported by Minard, et al (2015) and Miller (2015, 2015b) on event cross-document coreference, we presume that chains of discursive and descriptive events can be captured, albeit with difficulty at present (Laparra et al 2017). These chains would explicitly include the dynamic events like quoting, recounting, and describing, along with the dynamic events like identification, repatriation, and enumeration, along with stative events like dead and missing. A current challenge is that although these methods would appear to capture aspects relevant to Bruner's phenomenological framework, they do so idiosyncratically. For example, Simonson's Chambers and Jurafsky-inspired schemas can find frequently occurring narrative patterns in news corpora, but cannot address aspects like the canonicity of narrative structures and their breach. In stories of the 2004 Indian Ocean earthquake and tsunami, stories frequently exemplifying the canonical form of a natural disaster and the recovery of first world citizens in second or third-world contexts, the form is breached when the hard reality of the only possible method of identification, dental records, eclipses the particular impact of the event on a given first-world nation far from the event's epicenter.

At the heart of this research is an effort to understand the relationship among narrative form and audience engagement with complex stories in the context of journalism. It is with narratological details such as those described above that we might find answers to questions such as how do different weather events get covered, why do audiences respond to some coverage but not others, what kinds of canonical frames are relied upon for covering different types of weather events and disasters, and how the coverage of events might better align with the significance of those events. While current methods of schema extraction and narrative alignment are remarkable in their ability to identify canonical scripts, they may only accidentally capture aspects of narrative necessary for the answering of complex questions. Future work needs to go beyond measures of accuracy to canon such as the Narrative Cloze test to instead assess the relationship of canonicity and breach, and to quantify the extent to which narrative features, even ones as culturally and generically limited as the Proppian functions, are represented in annotations or extractions.

Our future work will be to conduct empirical research on our weather-event corpora to assess the efficacy of, first, cross-document narrative alignment using fuzzy matching of word embedding-based event chains, and second, to manually assess the extent to which that method indirect captures narrative features concordant with a blended Bruner-Genette framework. This position paper, by describing how that framework would support critical reading, interpretation, and inference of events in the news, makes the argument that events must be considered more as conceptual containers that incorporate the commonplace with its exception, than as linguistic tokens reflective of the common.

Acknowledgements

The author would like to thank Ayush Shrestha, Jennifer Olive, Yanjun Zhao, and Shakthidar Gopavaram, collaborators on prior research into narrative segmentation and alignment upon which this work builds. I would also like to thank the reviewers of this paper for their valuable feedback, in particular about morphological approaches to the narrative analysis of folktales, and the ongoing challenge of capturing narrative sequences.

References

Bagga, A., and Baldwin, B. (1999). "Cross-document event coreference: Annotations, experiments, and observations." *Proceedings of the Workshop on Coreference and its Applications*. Association for Computational Linguistics.

Bal, M. (1985). *Narratology: Introduction to the Study of Narrative*. Trans. Christine van Boheemen. Toronto: U of Toronto P.

Bean, D. L., & Riloff, E. (2004). Unsupervised Learning of Contextual Role Knowledge for Coreference Resolution. In *HLT-NAACL* (pp. 297-304).

Bruner, J. (1991). The narrative construction of reality. *Critical inquiry, 18*(1), 1-21.

Caselli, Tommaso, and Piek Vossen. "The Event StoryLine Corpus: A New Benchmark for Causal and Temporal Relation Extraction." *Proceedings of the Events and Stories in the News Workshop* (EventStory 2017). 2017

Chambers, N., & Jurafsky, D. (2008, June). Unsupervised Learning of Narrative Event Chains. In *ACL* (Vol. 94305, pp. 789-797).

Chambers, N., & Jurafsky, D. (2009). Unsupervised learning of narrative schemas and their participants. In *Proceedings of the Joint Conference of the 47th Annual Meeting of the ACL and the 4th International Joint Conference on Natural Language Processing of the AFNLP: Volume 2-Volume 2* (pp. 602-610). Association for Computational Linguistics.

Dundes, A. (1963). Structural Typology in North American Indian Folktales. *Southwestern Journal of Anthropology*, 19(1), 121-130.

Finlayson, M. A. (2015). Propplearner: Deeply annotating a corpus of Russian folktales to enable the machine learning of a Russian formalist theory. *Digital Scholarship in the Humanities*, fqv067.

Finlayson, M. A. (2016). Inferring Propp's functions from semantically annotated text. *Journal of American Folklore*, *129*(511), 55-77.

Fleming, J. (2014). Media literacy, news literacy, or news appreciation? A case study of the news literacy program at Stony Brook University. *Journalism & Mass Communication Educator*, *69*(2), 146-165.

Genette, G. (1980). *Narrative discourse* (JE Lewin, Trans.). Ithaca, NY: Cornell UP.

Genette, G. (1983). *Narrative discourse: An essay in method*. Cornell University Press.

Gervás, P. (2016). An Exploratory Model of Remembering, Telling and Understanding Experience in Simple Agents. In *Proceedings of the Workshop on Computational Creativity, Concept Invention, and General Intelligence (C3GI 2016)* Vol-1767. CEUR Workshop Proceedings.

Hornik, R. (2017). Why News Literacy Matters: A New Literacy for Civil Society in the 21st Century. Digital Resource Center.

Johnson-Laird, P. N. (1983). *Mental models: Towards a cognitive science of language, inference, and consciousness* (No. 6). Harvard University Press.

Laparra, E., Agerri, R., Aldabe, I., & Rigau, G. (2017). Multi-lingual and Cross-lingual timeline extraction. *Knowledge-Based Systems*, 133, 77-89.

Gilet, P. (1998). *Vladimir Propp and the Universal Folktale: Recommissioning an Old Paradigm--story as Initiation* (Vol. 17). Peter Lang Pub. Incorporated.

Gordon, J., Hobbs, J.R., May, J., et al. (2015). "A Corpus of Rich Metaphor Annotation". In *Proceedings of the Third Workshop on Metaphor in NLP*.

LDC. (2005). Ace (automatic content extraction) English annotation guidelines for events ver. 5.4.3 2005.07.01. Technical report, Linguistic Data Consortium

Lewis, D. (1978). Truth in fiction. *American Philosophical Quarterly*, *15*(1), 37-46.

Mani, I. (2014). Computational narratology. *Handbook of narratology*, 84-92.

Miller, B., Shrestha, A. & Subtirelu, N. (2014) "NLP Approaches to Rights Violation Classifying." Paper presented at the annual *RightsCon meeting*, San Francisco, California.

Miller, B., Shrestha, A., Olive, J., & Gopavaram, S. (2015). Cross-Document Narrative Frame Alignment. In *OASIcs-OpenAccess Series in Informatics* (Vol. 45). Schloss Dagstuhl-Leibniz-Zentrum fuer Informatik.

Miller, B., Olive, J., Gopavaram, S., et al. (2015b). A method for cross-document narrative alignment of a two-hundred-sixty-million word corpus. In *Big Data (Big Data), 2015 IEEE International Conference on* (pp. 1673-1677). IEEE.

Minard, A. L., Speranza, M., Agirre, E., Aldabe, I., van Erp, M., Magnini, B., ... & Urizar, R. (2015). Semeval-2015 task 4: Timeline: Cross-document event ordering. In *9th International Workshop on Semantic Evaluation (SemEval 2015)* (pp. 778-786).

O'Gorman, T., Wright-Bettner, K., & Palmer, M. (2016). Richer Event Description: Integrating event coreference with temporal, causal and bridging annotation. *Computing News Storylines*, 47.

Gervás, P. (2013). Propp's Morphology of the Folk Tale as a Grammar for Generation. In *Proceedings of the 2013 Workshop on Computational Models of Narrative*, Dagstuhl, Germany

Ponti, E. M., & Korhonen, A. (2017). Event-Related Features in Feedforward Neural Networks Contribute to Identifying Causal Relations in Discourse. *LSDSem 2017*, 25.

Pustejovsky, J., Hanks, P., Sauri, R. et al. (2003, March). The timebank corpus. In *Corpus linguistics* (Vol. 2003, p. 40).

Ryan, M. L. (1991). *Possible worlds, artificial intelligence, and narrative theory*. Indiana University Press.

Segers, R., Vossen, P., Rospocher, M., Serafini, L., Laparra, E., & Rigau, G. (2015). Eso: A frame based ontology for events and implied situations. *Proceedings of Maplex 2015.*

Shklovsky, V. (1991) *Theory of Prose*, trans. B. Sher, Intr. G.L. Burns. Elmwood Park, IL: Dalkey Archive Press.

Simonson, D., & Davis, A. (2016). NASTEA: Investigating Narrative Schemas through Annotated Entities. *Computing News Storylines*, 57.

Simonson, D., Davis, A. R., & Solutions, E. (2015). Interactions between Narrative Schemas and Document Categories. *ACL-IJCNLP 2015*, 1.

Sprugnoli, R., & Tonelli, S. (2016). One, no one and one hundred thousand events: Defining and processing events in an inter-disciplinary perspective. *Natural Language Engineering*, 1-22.

Propp, V. (1968). *Morphology of The Folk Tale* (second edition). University of Texas Press.

Vossen, P., & Cybulska, A. (2017). Identity and Granularity of Events in Text. *arXiv preprint arXiv:1704.04259.*

Identifying the Discourse Function of News Article Paragraphs

W. Victor H. Yarlott[1], **Cristina Cornelio**[2], **Tian Gao**[2], **Mark A. Finlayson**[1]

[1]School of Computing and Information Sciences
Florida International University, Miami, FL 33199
`wvyar@cs.fiu.edu, markaf@fiu.edu`

[2]IBM T.J. Watson Research Center
Yorktown Heights, NY 10598
`{ccornel, tgao}@us.ibm.com`

Abstract

Discourse structure is a key aspect of all forms of text, providing valuable information both to humans and machines. We applied the hierarchical theory of news discourse developed by van Dijk (1988) to examine how paragraphs operate as units of discourse structure within news articles—what we refer to here as *document-level discourse*. This document-level discourse provides a characterization of the content of each paragraph that describes its relation to the events presented in the article (such as *main events*, *backgrounds*, and *consequences*) as well as to other components of the story (such as *commentary* and *evaluation*). The purpose of a news discourse section is of great utility to story understanding as it affects both the importance and temporal order of items introduced in the text—therefore, if we know the news discourse purpose for different sections, we should be able to better rank events for their importance and better construct timelines. We test two hypotheses: first, that people can reliably annotate news articles with van Dijk's theory; second, that we can reliably predict these labels using machine learning. We show that people have a high degree of agreement with each other when annotating the theory ($F_1 > 0.8$, $\kappa > 0.6$), demonstrating that it can be both learned and reliably applied by human annotators. Additionally, we demonstrate first steps toward machine learning of the theory, achieving a performance of $F_1 = 0.54$, which is 65% of human performance. Moreover, we have generated a gold-standard, adjudicated corpus of 50 documents for document-level discourse annotation based on the ACE Phase 2 corpus (NIST, 2002).

1 Introduction

Discourse structure is a key aspect of all forms of text, providing valuable information about the contents of a given span of text. This is most obvious in academic, legal, and technical texts, which are often clearly delineated into sections containing, for example, introductory, background, or explanatory material, among others—these type of texts are designed to make it easy to find specific information within them quickly. News articles have a similarly helpful, though implicit, design: they often provide a brief, up-front summary of the important events, relevant background information, comments from both experts and the reporters, and detailed descriptions of the main events. Events are often not presented in chronological order, but rather structured by importance.

We use an established hierarchical theory of news discourse (van Dijk, 1988) to model how paragraphs operate as units of discourse structure within news articles to capture the importance of events within a story. We test two hypotheses: first, that humans can reliably annotate news articles with van Dijk's theory; second, that these discourse labels can be predicted by machine learning.

In our first hypothesis, by *reliable* we specifically mean that independent people agree with each other when applying van Dijk's theory of news discourse. We performed an annotation study to answer this question, producing a small corpus of gold-standard, adjudicated annotations in a standoff format based on the Automated Content Extraction (ACE) Phase 2 corpus (NIST, 2002). This corpus consists of 50 documents (28,236 words; 644 paragraphs) annotated at the paragraph level. Agreement was notable, with $F_1 > 0.75$ and Cohen's $\kappa > 0.60$ (see §4.3 for details). These results show that van Dijk's theory of can be both learned and reliably applied by humans to news article.

Proceedings of the Workshop on Events and Stories in the News, pages 25–33
Santa Fe, New Mexico, USA, August 20, 2018.

To address our second hypothesis, we demonstrate a machine learning approach using support vector machine (SVM) for learning to tag paragraphs with labels from van Dijk's theory. We achieve a performance of $F_1 = 0.54$, which is 65% of human performance. We also demonstrate the performance of other machine learning algorithms (decision tree and random forest) and provide the set of features that perform the best on this task.

The paper is structured as follows. We first introduce some of the existing related work (§2), and then provide a definition of van Dijk's theory as was presented to our annotators (§3). We next describe the selection of texts used in this study, provide corpus statistics, describe the training and annotation procedures for the study, and describe the results of the annotation study and provide some discussion on these results (§4). We then provide an automated method to learn and predict the discourse-structure labels of a plain document (§5), followed by discussion on the results of label prediction and some remarks of possible future directions (§6). Finally, we summarize our contributions (§7).

2   Related Work

There has been a substantial work describing how the structure of news operates with regards to the chronology of real-world events. Much news follows an inverted chronology—called the inverted pyramid (Bell, 1998; Delin, 2000) or relevance ordering (Van Dijk, 1986)—where the most important and typically the most recent events come first. Bell claims that *"news stories... are seldom if ever told in chronological order"* (Bell, 1994, p. 105), which is demonstrated by Rafiee *et al.* for both Western (Dutch) and non-Western (Iranian) news (2017). Rafiee *et al.* also show that many stories follow a hybrid structure, which combines characteristics from both inverted and chronological structures.

In this work, we focus on van Dijk's structural approach to the structure of news discourse (van Dijk, 1988), which is organized as a tree. We choose this work as our focus due to the presentation and description of the schemata, which facilitated the quick development of an annotation guide. A more in-depth description of van Dijk's theory is presented in Section 3.

Discussing van Dijk's theory of news discourse, Bekalu states that analysis of *"the processes involved in the production of news discourses and their structures will ultimately derive their relevance from our insights into the consequences, effects, or functions for readers in different social contexts, which obviously leads us to a consideration of news comprehension"* (2006, p. 150). The theory proposed by van Dijk has also been proposed for use in annotating the global structure of elementary discourse units in Dutch news articles (van der Vliet et al., 2011).

Pan and Kosicki (1993), in a similar analysis, present a framing-based approach that provides four structural dimensions for the analysis of news discourse: syntactic structure, script structure, thematic structure, and rhetorical structure. Of these, the syntactic structure is most closely aligned with van Dijk's theory. In this paper, we chose to focus on van Dijk's theory as Pan and Kosicki do not provide a list or description of the structure that could be readily translated into an annotation scheme.

White (1998) treats the structure of news as being centered around the headline and lead. White suggests that the headline and lead, which act as a combination of both synopsis and abstract for the news story, serve as the nucleus for the rest of the text: *"the body which follows the headline/lead nucleus—acts to specify the meanings presented in the opening headline/lead nucleus through elaboration, contextualisation, explanation, and appraisal"* (1998, p. 275). We focus on van Dijk's theory for this paper as we find it to provide a higher degree of specificity: White's specification modes serve roughly the same purpose as higher-level groupings in van Dijk's theory.

For this work, we use the ACE Phase 2 corpus (NIST, 2002) as the source of our news articles. We choose this corpus because it fit three criteria: it is a widely-used news corpus, it has relevance to other tasks (entity detection and relation detection), and it was readily available to us.

3   Van Dijk's Theory of News Discourse

Van Dijk (1988) provides a hierarchical theory of news discourse, shown in Figure 1, which we apply to a subset of the news articles of the ACE Phase 2 corpus. In this section, we briefly describe the leaf categories as well as their parent categories when appropriate. We provide additional annotation details for discourse types where van Dijk's description appeared underspecified, as we have done in the guide given to our annotators.

Summary elements express the major subject of the article, with the *headline* being a special construct that introduces a topic, and the *lead* summarizing the topic introduced by the headline. While annotators were initially instructed to annotate the headline, we do not include it in our annotations, as the ACE Phase 2 corpus has the headline separate as part of its annotation scheme.

Situation elements are the actual events that comprise the major subject of the article. *Episodes* concern *main events*, which are those events that directly relate to the major subject of the article, and the *consequences* of those events. The *background* consists of the *context*, which are any *circumstances* that contribute to understanding the subject as well as any *previous events*. Where circumstances may be non-specific, previous events refer to a specific event that has occurred recently. *History* elements are those events that have not occurred recently, typically referenced in terms of years prior, rather than months, weeks, or days. These elements of the discourse structure provide important information about the relation of each paragraph with respect to the central events of a news story.

Conclusions are those *comments* made by the journalistic entity (the newspaper, reporter, etc.) regarding the subject. These can be *expectations* about the resolution or consequences of an event, or *evaluations* of the current situation. In contrast, *verbal reactions* are *comments* solicited from an external source, such as a person involved in the events of the article, an expert, etc. These elements of the discourse provide further supporting context for the central events of an article.

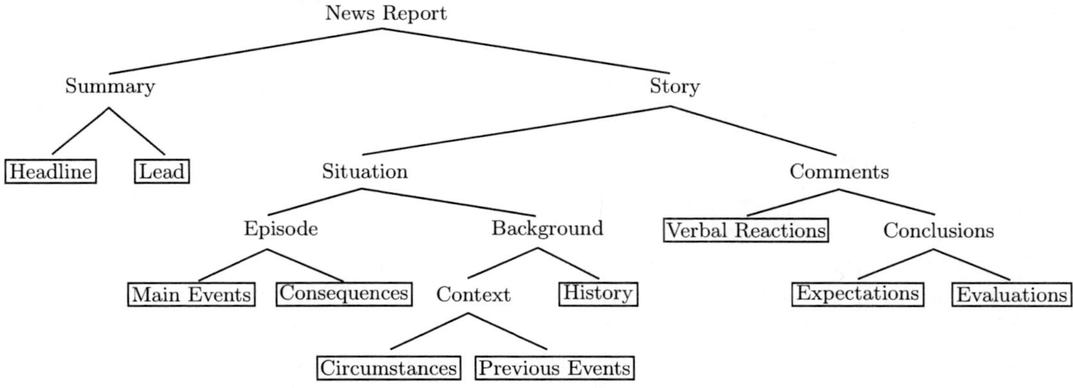

Figure 1: The hierarchical discourse structure of news proposed by van Dijk (van Dijk, 1988).

4 Data & Annotation

One of the major contributions of this paper is the generation of a gold-standard corpus of document-level discourse structure based on the existing ACE Phase 2 corpus. This new dataset comprises 50 documents containing 28,236 words divided in 644 paragraphs. This annotation is, to the best of knowledge, the first of this kind, and provides additional information about the corpus that, until now, is not considered in any knowledge extraction method. We provide, in the following sections, the details of our corpus.

4.1 Selection of Texts

We selected the ACE Phase 2 corpus because it is a major standard corpora of news articles that satisfied three criteria: it is widely-used, has relevance to other tasks, and was readily available to us. We annotated 50 randomly selected news articles from the development set, divided into ten sets of five documents each. Within these sets, documents were swapped or replaced in order to obtain uniform sets in terms of total document lengths. Table 1 shows the corpus-wide statistics for the number of words and paragraphs, where each paragraph is given a single type in accordance to van Dijk's theory. The majority of texts were already divided into paragraphs in an obvious manner, either with empty lines or with indentation.

The remaining texts were divided by the adjudicator based on either contextual or structural clues, such as abrupt change in topic or unnatural line breaks.

	Words	Paragraphs
Total	28,236	644
Average	564.7	12.9
Standard Deviation	322.1	4.9

Table 1: Corpus-wide statistics on the relevant lexical features for annotating the news articles.

4.2 Annotation

Annotation was done in a double-blind manner by three annotators, one of whom also acted as the adjudicator. All three annotators are Ph.D. students in computer science with a focus on natural language processing, with experience in both annotating and running annotation studies.

4.2.1 Annotator Training

The annotators that took part in this project were given minimal training outside of their individual experience with annotation studies. Annotators were provided with a guide describing van Dijk's theory. A single adjudication meeting was held after annotation for the first two sets of documents was completed. The primary purpose of this adjudication meeting was to resolve any questions the annotators had, discover any uncertainty in the annotation guide, and revise the annotation guide to address these questions. The annotation guide contains descriptions of each discourse label in addition to an example of a fully-annotated news article, shown in Figure 2.

4.2.2 Annotation Procedure

Annotation was performed over the course of a month, as time allowed. The adjudicator performed annotation of all ten sets of documents, while the other two annotators performed annotation of six sets each. Figure 3 illustrates this division of work. Annotation of each set took approximately 45 minutes to an hour, resulting in roughly ten hours of annotation work for the adjudicator and six hours for the other two annotators. The annotations were performed using Microsoft Word's built-in comment feature, to eliminate the need for any tool-based annotator training. When confronted with multiple labels that seemed to fit, annotators were instructed to choose the label that seemed the most applicable.

The adjudication procedure took a further hour for each set of documents, resulting in another ten hours of work for the adjudicator and another two hours for the other two annotators, who were only required to participate in adjudication of the first two sets of documents. The purpose of this group adjudication meeting was to resolve any outstanding questions or confusions regarding the annotation procedure. The annotation resulted in triple annotation for the first ten documents, and double annotation for the remaining forty documents. The multiple annotations were merged into a gold standard for every document. Additionally, although annotators were instructed to annotate the headline for each document, these labels are not included as part of the gold standard because within the ACE Phase 2 dataset, the headlines themselves are clearly annotated.

4.3 Annotation Results

This annotation study had two goals: first, to produce a benchmark dataset of document-level discourse annotations to evaluate the impact of document-level discourse on information extraction. Second, to evaluate whether or not humans can reliably apply van Dijk's theory to actual documents. By *reliable* we mean that annotators have a high degree of agreement with respect to each other. To measure agreement, we use the standard F_1 score (van Rijsbergen, 1979), treating one of the annotators as the correct labels, as well as Cohen's kappa coefficient for inter-rater agreement (Cohen, 1968).

The results of the annotation study are shown in Table 2. Inter-annotator agreement between annotators A1 and A2 was measured over ten documents; inter-annotator agreement between the annotators and the

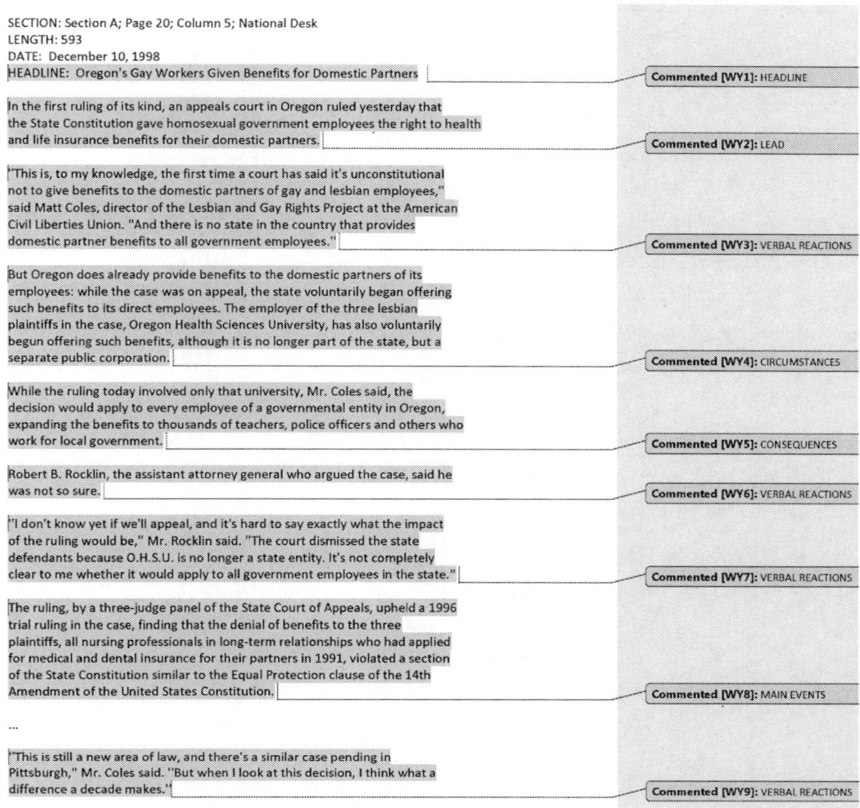

Figure 2: Example annotation included in the annotation guide. Some parts of the annotation have been omitted for brevity.

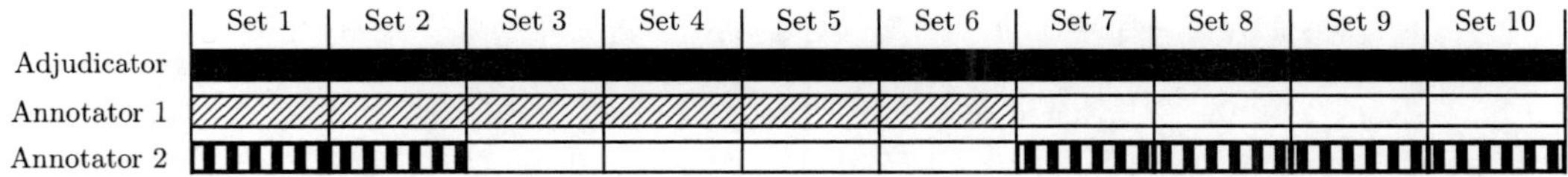

Figure 3: Division of work for the annotation study.

adjudicator, as well as the annotators and the gold standard, was measured over 30 documents. The comparison between the adjudicator and the gold standard was measured over the entire collection of 50 documents.

Table 3 provides the distribution of van Dijk's labels (sans headlines, of which there are 50: one for each document, annotated within the ACE Phase 2 corpus). Verbal reactions and circumstances dominate the labels.

4.3.1 Discussion

We observed that the inter-annotator agreement between the adjudicator and the individual annotators is high ($F_1 = 0.8$, $\kappa = 0.6$). Moreover, the results in Table 2 indicate that annotators, even with minimal training, can reliably apply van Dijk's theory.

Inter-annotator agreement between the two annotators is also high, although lower than agreement with the adjudicator ($F_1 = 0.75$, $\kappa = 0.5$). One possible reason is that the adjudicator was also responsible for the annotation guide: since the adjudicator is the source of the initial examples and instructions for

Comparison	# Docs	P	R	F_1	p_0	p_e	κ
A1 vs. A2	10	0.76	0.79	0.77	0.63	0.18	0.55
Adj. vs. A1	30	0.81	0.85	0.83	0.71	0.19	0.64
Adj. vs. A2	30	0.80	0.83	0.82	0.69	0.18	0.62
A1 vs. Gold	30	0.93	0.92	0.92	0.86	0.19	0.83
A2 vs. Gold	30	0.92	0.90	0.91	0.83	0.19	0.80
Adj. vs. Gold	50	0.93	0.87	0.90	0.81	0.18	0.77

Table 2: Microaveraged agreement measures between the annotators (A1, A2), adjudicator (Adj.), and the merged gold standard (Gold)—including precision (P), recall (R), balanced F-measure (F_1), relative observed agreement among raters (p_0), probability of chance agreement (p_e), and Cohen's kappa (κ, derived from p_0 and p_e).

Label	Count
Lead	42
Main	60
Consequences	19
Circumstances	103
Previous Events	64
History	27
Verbal Reactions	252
Expectations	21
Evaluations	56
Total	644

Table 3: Distribution of the labels within the annotated corpus. The majority of paragraphs fall under the categories of verbal reactions or circumstances.

annotation, is reasonable that the annotators would agree more strongly with the adjudicator than with each other.

Comparisons with the gold-standard are included for completeness: the all-around high agreement with the gold standard ($F_1 = 0.85$, $\kappa = 0.75$) demonstrate that the gold-standard is not dominated by a single annotator.

Although the distribution of labels is highly skewed, we find that this is roughly in-line with the style of reporting featured in the ACE Phase 2 corpus, which seeks comments and analysis from experts within the field as well as explaining the immediate context that has an effect on the main event.

5 Discourse Label Prediction

We build on top of our annotation study to demonstrate the automated learning of document-level discourse on a per-paragraph basis. We use machine learning algorithms included in Scikit-learn (Pedregosa et al., 2011) for our classifiers: in particular, we use the `svm.SVC` implementation of support vector machines (SVM), the `tree.DecisionTreeClassifier` implementation of decision trees, and the `ensemble.RandomForestClassifier` implementation of random forests. We include decision tree and random forest results despite their lower performance because they are particularly interesting for this experiment, as the theory itself is hierarchical. In addition to features from Scikit-learn, we also use the paragraph vectors (Mikolov et al., 2013) implementation in Gensim (Řehůřek and Sojka, 2010).

5.1 Feature Selection

In this section, we briefly describe the features we use and explain our rationale behind them.

Bag of Words We use Scikit-learn's `text.CountVectorizer` class with the standard English stop-words to provide a count of the tokens in each paragraph. This feature was selected based on the idea that paragraphs from different types of discourse would use different language.

TF-IDF We use Scikit-learn's `text.TfidfTransformer` class with standard parameters. TF-IDF was selected as one method to approximate topics within a given paragraph.

Paragraph Vectors We use Gensim's `models.doc2vec.Doc2Vec` class using the distributed bag-of-words model, with a minimum α of 0.01, a minimum word occurrence of five, and 50 steps (`dm=0, min_alpha=0.01, min_count=5, steps=50`). We use this as a second method of approximating the topic of a given paragraph.

Previous Paragraph's Label We also include the label from the previous paragraph. This feature is based on the idea that there is, to some degree, some sequential ordering or restriction in discourse type. One simple example is that a lead paragraph is never followed by another lead paragraph.

The bag of words, TF-IDF, and paragraph vector models are built across the entire training corpus and roughly measure what topics and words correspond to specific label types.

5.2 Results

Our best experimental results were obtained using grid search to maximize the micro-averaged performance of the classifier, as measured across five folds. The SVM classifier uses a linear kernel with $C = 10$ and the class weights balanced based on the training data; the decision tree classifier uses the default parameters with the class weights balanced; the random forest uses 50 estimators with balanced class weights.

Feature Groups	P	R	F_1
Baseline #1 (Most Freq. Class)	0.39	0.39	0.39
Baseline #2 (SVM + Bag of Words)	0.46	0.46	0.46
Decision Tree	0.41	0.41	0.41
Random Forest	0.43	0.43	0.43
SVM	0.54	0.54	**0.54**

Table 4: Results from label prediction using SVM. All results are micro-averaged across instances, including precision (P), recall (R), and balanced F-measure (F_1). For the final three classifiers, all four features are described in §5.1.

Table 4 presents the results from our experiments, showing that our classifier is a substantial improvement over the most-frequent-class and bag-of-words baselines. We note that because these features are fairly generic, and do not include potentially more informative and semantically and syntactically rich features (such as, e.g., event-, coreference-, dialog-, or discourse-specific features), these results give us hope of much better performance with further experimentation.

Table 5 presents the per-label results from our experiments. The relatively strong performance on *circumstances* and *verbal reactions* is not surprising, given their predominance. Similarly it is not surprising that we have low performance on labels that occur, on average, about once a document. We observe an unexpected level of performance on *lead* paragraphs, given their relative scarceness in the dataset. Within the data, we find that leads, with a single exception, occur at the start of the document: this accounts for the high performance, given that the first paragraph's previous paragraph is represented as -1, allowing the classifier to take advantage of their strong positional tendency.

6 Discussion

We find that using our SVM classifier, we achieve reasonable performance (65% of human performance). We suspect that an increase in performance can be gained by additional feature engineering. Moreover,

Label Type	F_1
Lead	0.87
Main	0.23
Consequences	0.13
Circumstances	0.46
Previous Events	0.18
History	0.05
Verbal Reactions	0.76
Expectations	0.08
Evaluations	0.19

Table 5: Per-label F_1 results. Best performance occurs for the lead, circumstances, and verbal reactions.

we expect that including high-precision rule-based prediction will further improve the performance of the system: this is based on comments during adjudication from annotators, who stated that they relied heavily on lexical clues such as quotation marks and specific words ("said," "commented," etc.) to select certain categories (in this case, *verbal reactions*).

While we expected the tree-oriented methods—decision trees and random forests—to outperform the SVM classifier, this was not the case in practice and they were outperformed by one of the baselines. We believe that this is because the features currently used fail to capture the higher-level semantic ideas that van Dijk used to group together the discourse types. While people understand that verbal reactions from experts, expectations, and evaluations are all types of comments, our current features do not capture these relations.

We anticipate several avenues for future work: first, there is much to be explored towards improving the performance of discourse label prediction; second, high-performance discourse label prediction enables the creation of larger corpora using automated methods; finally, following our annotation model, we anticipate further work in discourse-based corpora.

We also believe that we can improve performance on specific under-performing label types by implementing high-precision classification rules to be applied prior to statistical classification, and annotating additional data with these under-performing types to obtain further representation of them within the dataset. Furthermore, we currently do not exploit the hierarchical nature of van Dijk's theory: doing so may provide additional performance gain by allowing specific classifiers for higher-level types.

7   Contributions

In this paper, we made several key contributions. First, we have demonstrated that humans can reliably learn and annotate news articles with van Dijk's theory of news discourse with a high degree of agreement. Second, we have developed a system that can predict the document-level discourse labels for paragraphs within a news article with reasonable performance (65% of human performance). Third, we have generated a gold-standard corpus of these labels, along with an annotation guide, to support future work.

Given that our corpus is based on the ACE Phase 2 data, this work will provide a foundation for interesting discoure-based approaches to information in news, provide a benchmark for testing extraction of document-level discourse extraction, and promote research related to discourse and the news. While entity detection and relation detection are directly supported by the corpus, we also see connections to event detection and coreference given the event-central nature of van Dijk's theory.

8   Acknowledgments

This research was made possible by an FIU's Presidential Fellowship and FIU's SCIS's Director's Fellowship, both awarded to Victor Yarlott. This work was also partially supported by Office of Naval Research award # N00014-17-1-2983. We would like to thank our two annotators, Deya Banisakher and

Joshua Eisenberg, for their hard work and attention to detail.

References

Mesfin Awoke Bekalu. 2006. Presupposition in news discourse. *Discourse & Society*, 17(2):147–172.

Allan Bell. 1994. Telling stories. *Media texts: Authors and readers*, pages 100–118.

Allan Bell. 1998. The discourse structure of news stories. *Approaches to media discourse*, pages 64–104.

Jacob Cohen. 1968. Weighted kappa: Nominal scale agreement provision for scaled disagreement or partial credit. *Psychological bulletin*, 70(4):213.

Judy Delin. 2000. *The language of everyday life: An introduction*. Sage.

Tomas Mikolov, Ilya Sutskever, Kai Chen, Greg S Corrado, and Jeff Dean. 2013. Distributed representations of words and phrases and their compositionality. In *Advances in neural information processing systems*, pages 3111–3119.

NIST. 2002. Ace phase 2.

Zhongdang Pan and Gerald M Kosicki. 1993. Framing analysis: An approach to news discourse. *Political communication*, 10(1):55–75.

Fabian Pedregosa, Gaël Varoquaux, Alexandre Gramfort, Vincent Michel, Bertrand Thirion, Olivier Grisel, Mathieu Blondel, Peter Prettenhofer, Ron Weiss, Vincent Dubourg, Jake Vanderplas, Alexandre Passos, David Cournapeau, Matthieu Brucher, Matthieu Perrot, and Édouard Duchesnay. 2011. Scikit-learn: Machine learning in Python. *Journal of Machine Learning Research*, 12:2825–2830.

Afrooz Rafiee, Wilbert Spooren, and José Sanders. 2017. Culture and discourse structure: A comparative study of dutch and iranian news texts. *Discourse & Communication*, page 1750481317735626.

Radim Řehůřek and Petr Sojka. 2010. Software Framework for Topic Modelling with Large Corpora. In *Proceedings of the LREC 2010 Workshop on New Challenges for NLP Frameworks*, pages 45–50, Valletta, Malta, May. ELRA. http://is.muni.cz/publication/884893/en.

Nynke van der Vliet, Ildikó Berzlánovich, Gosse Bouma, Markus Egg, and Gisela Redeker. 2011. Building a discourse-annotated dutch text corpus. *Bochumer Linguistische Arbeitsberichte*, 3:157–171.

Teun A Van Dijk, 1986. *Studying Writing: Linguistic Approaches. Written Communication Annual: An International Survey of Research and Theory Series, Volume 1.*, chapter News Schemata, pages 155–185. ERIC.

Teun A van Dijk, 1988. *News as Discourse*, chapter Structure of News, pages 52–57. Lawrence Erlbaum Associates, Inc., Hillsdale, New Jersey.

Cornelis J. van Rijsbergen. 1979. *Information retrieval*. Butterworths, London Boston.

Peter R White. 1998. *Telling media tales: The news story as rhetoric*. Department of Linguistics, Faculty of Arts, University of Sydney.

An Evaluation of Information Extraction Tools for Identifying Health Claims in News Headlines

Shi Yuan
School of Economics and Management
Beihang University
Beijing, China
`ystone1025@buaa.edu.cn`

Bei Yu
School of Information Studies
Syracuse University
Syracuse, NY, USA
`byu@syr.edu`

Abstract

This study evaluates the performance of four information extraction tools (extractors) on identifying health claims in health news headlines. A health claim is defined as a triplet: IV (what is being manipulated), DV (what is being measured) and their relation. Tools that can identify health claims provide the foundation for evaluating the accuracy of these claims against authoritative resources. The evaluation result shows that 26% headlines do not include health claims, and all extractors face difficulty separating them from the rest. For those with health claims, OPENIE-5.0 performed the best with F-measure at 0.6 level for extracting "IV-relation-DV". However, the characteristic linguistic structures in health news headlines, such as incomplete sentences and non-verb relations, pose particular challenge to existing tools.

1 Introduction

Mass media is a major source of information about health-related research, policies, and business. On average, four in ten American adults reported following health news stories closely. Thus, the quality of health news plays an important role in public understanding of health science (Brodie et al., 2003). However, inaccuracy in health news has raised concerns among scientists, journalists, and the general public. The lack of training has been identified as the main cause of low-quality health news stories (Sarri et al., 1998; Voss, 2002).

This study aims for using NLP techniques to identify inaccuracy in health news reporting. The resulting tools may be used for monitoring the quality of health news and providing training examples for journalists and readers. To achieve this ultimate goal, we propose a two-step solution: first extract the health claims in news stories and then verify these claims against reliable sources, such as original research publications. In this study we focus on the first step to extract health claims from news headlines, because headlines serve the role of attracting readers to click and read the whole story (NPR, 2018), and thus the inaccuracies in headlines may be more consequential than those in the main stories.

FDA (2009) defined a health claim as "the relationship between a substance and a disease or health-related condition". Sumner et al. (2014) defined it more broadly as a triplet of three elements: Independent Variable (IV), Dependent Variable (DV), and their relation. IV is defined as what is being manipulated, DV as what is being measured, and relation as the words that describe the link between IV and DV. They have applied this definition for manually examining exaggerations in health-related claims in science publications, press releases and news articles. Therefore, we adopt this definition to represent health claims. For example, in the headline *"Drug suppresses spread of breast cancer caused by stem-like cells"*, the "IV-relation-DV" is *"drug; suppresses; spread of breast cancer"*.

Entity-relation extraction has been a fundamental task in the area of information extraction. Some general-purpose tools have been developed to extract entities and relations, such as OPENIE-5.0 (Mausam, 2016), OLLIE (Mausam et al., 2012) and REVERB (Fader et al., 2011; Etzioni et al., 2011). Some tools were developed for specific domains, such as SemRep for extracting relations in biomedical publications (Rindflesch and Marcelo, 2003). However, the health news headlines sometimes have

Proceedings of the Workshop on Events and Stories in the News, pages 34–43
Santa Fe, New Mexico, USA, August 20, 2018.

unique grammatical structures compared to regular sentences with "subject-predicate-object" structures. For example, the noun *"prevalence"* describes the relation in the headline *"Prevalence of estrogen receptor mutations in patients with metastatic breast cancer"*. Therefore, existing information extraction tools may encounter challenges in identifying "IV-relation-DV" from health news headlines.

In this paper, we evaluate popular information extraction tools for identifying health claims in the format of "IV-relation-DV" triples in health news headlines. The result is expected to shed light on the directions for improving the existing tools. The rest of paper is organized as follows. Section 2 reviews the state-of-the-art information extraction tools. Section 3 describes the construction of the benchmark data set. Section 4 presents the evaluation methods and results. Section 5 discusses the challenges that current tools face and offers suggestions for adaptation. Section 6 concludes the paper.

2 Related Work on Entity-relation Extraction

Studies in open information extraction aim for recognizing general-purpose "subject-relation-object" triplets from text. Based on the order of entity and relation identification, existing methods can be summarized into three types: identify entities first and then relations, identify relations first and then entities, and simultaneously identify both.

The first type of studies identifies entities first and then specifies some patterns to extract relations. REXTOR (Katz and Lin, 2000) is an early system that uses grammar rules for entity and relation extraction. Later, WOE^{Parse} (Wu and Weld, 2010), trained on Wikipedia articles, used dependency route patterns to decide whether two entities have relations. Besides, Relnoun (Pal and Mausam, 2016) was developed to extract relations from compound noun phrases, such as *"Collins; be director of; NIH"* in *"Collins, the director of NIH"*. The designs of these methods raise some questions regarding their adaptability to our task. For REXTOR, the grammar rules would link entities to several types of relations that do not apply to our task, such as "is subject of". WOE^{Parse} would match entities to what appear in Wikipedia; however, IVs and DVs in our task may be new and thus not yet included in Wikipedia. For Relnoun, health claims in our task are not usually expressed in compound noun phrases.

Different from the first method, some studies prefer recognizing relations first. For example, REVERB (Fader et al., 2011; Etzioni et al., 2011) first extracts the longest word sequence that satisfies certain syntactic and lexical constraints as a relation. It then searches for the entities as two noun phrases that are nearest to the relation phrase, one on left, one on right. Experiment results have shown that REVERB has 30% higher AUC than WOE^{Parse} based on the precision-recall curve (Etzioni et al., 2011). Similar to REVERB, SRLIE (Christensen et al., 2011) is also a verb-centric system. It first identifies all verbs and their modifiers, and then extracts the verbs with at least two modifiers as relations. However, REVERB may mistakenly identify modifiers to IVs and DVs as entities when they are closer to the relation verbs. In Comparison, SRLIE tends to ignore the modifiers to IVs and DVs.

The third method is designed for simultaneously identifying entities and relations. This method usually depends on "subject-relation-object" patterns. For example, OLLIE (Mausam et al., 2012) uses dependency parsing patterns to identify triplets. Before OLLIE, TEXTRUNNER (Banko et al., 2007), a CRF-based system, uses part-of-speech tags for triplet identification. Empirical results showed that OLLIE performed better than REVERB based on precision-yield curve (Mausam et al., 2012), and REVERB better than TEXTRUNNER based on precision-recall curve (Etzioni et al., 2011). Furthermore, considering the need for identifying numerical relations, BONIE (Saha et al., 2017) applied numerical dependency patterns to extract triplets that a number or a quantity-unit phrase, such as *"Hong Kong; has labour force of; 3.5 million"* in *"Hong Kong's labour force is 3.5 million"*.

Based on OLLIE, a new generation extractor named OPENIE-5.0 has been developed (Mausam, 2016). It combined SRLIE, Relnoun, BONIE and ListExtraction (Extraction from conjunctive sentences). Compared by precision-yield curve, OPENIE-5.0 is better than both OLLIE and REVERB (Mausam, 2016).

Overall, the aforementioned extractors rely on structural information in complete sentences to identify triplets. However, news headlines are often times not complete sentences. Therefore, whether the applicability of these extractors remain an open question.

In addition, because health news involves many biomedical concepts, we also reviewed information extractors in the biomedicine domain. SemRep (Rindflesch and Marcelo, 2003) is the state-of-the-art tool to identify semantic predications from biomedical text. It is a widely-used, rule-based system. The rules were derived from phrase structures (e.g., appositive structures). Furthermore, SemRep also relies on UMLS, a biomedical knowledge database, to identify concepts and relations. Besides SemRep, Dey et al. (2007) also proposed a system, which summarized PubMed articles by combining entity-relation structures into a network. The method for entity-relation structure identification depends on dependency relation rules. In comparison, SemRep suits our task better because the goal of Dey et al. (2007) is for text summarization instead of information extraction.

Based on the above review of the strength and weakness of the information extraction tools, we choose to evaluate four tools that best suit our task for extracting "IV-relation-DV" triplets in health news headlines: two representative systems of different methods (REVERB and OLLIE), a combination system (OPENIE-5.0) and a specific tool tailored to biomedicine (SemRep).

3   Benchmark Dataset Construction

We created a benchmark data set for evaluating the information extraction tools. This section describes the process of data collection, annotation, and validation.

3.1   Data Collection

`ScienceDaily.com` is a large website that aggregates science news. We collected all health news from `ScienceDaily.com` in 2016 and 2017, and selected all news articles with headlines including two common diseases "breast cancer" and "diabetes". The final collection contains 564 news articles, including 212 news headlines on breast cancer and 352 on diabetes. Those news headlines have been all annotated health claims manually.

3.2   Data Annotation Schema

We developed an annotation schema that includes three types of health claims: the first type does not describe a health claim, the second type describes a health claim between an IV and a DV, and the third type describes a health claim among multiple quasi-IVs (Sumner et al., 2014). Specifically, we define the annotation schema as:

- Health Claim or Not: Label a headline as "1" if it describes a health claim, otherwise label "0". For example, the headline *"Diabetics who use verapamil have lower glucose levels, data show"* is labeled as "1", but the headline *"Better breast cancer drugs?"* is labeled as "0". Sometimes health claims are phrased as questions in headlines, such as *"Can mindful eating help lower risk of type 2 diabetes, cardiovascular disease?"* For such cases, we also label them as "1".

- IV: What is being manipulated, e.g., *"Fasting-mimicking diet"* is the IV in the headline *"Fasting-mimicking diet may reverse diabetes"*. The annotated IV should include all relevant words, including the modifiers. For example, the IV of *"Teen girls with a family history of breast cancer do not experience increased depression or anxiety"* is *"Teen girls with a family history of breast cancer"*. Label "0" if no IV is found.

- DV: What is being measured, e.g., *"diabetes"* in in the headline *"Fasting-mimicking diet may reverse diabetes"*. Label "0" if no DV is found. Similar to the IV annotation, the annotated DV should include all relevant modifiers. For example, the DV of *"Smoking can hamper common treatment for breast cancer"* is *"common treatment for breast cancer"*.

- Relation: The statement of relation between IV and DV. The annotated relation should include all modifiers, like modal verbs (e.g., *"can"*), negative words (e.g., *"not"*), preposition combinations (e.g., *"associated with"*) and verb combinations (e.g., *"help reduce"*). For example, the relation is *"found to switch"* in *"Breast cancer cells found to switch molecular characteristics"*.

- Multiple IVs: Sometimes multiple quasi-IVs were mentioned if they are correlated (Sumner et al., 2014). In these cases, they are described in the same phrase, and thus impossible to separate as two independent phrases. For example, *"heart hormones, obesity, and diabetes"* in the headline *"New links between heart hormones, obesity, and diabetes"*.

3.3 Inter-coder Agreement

We randomly chose 100 news headlines to evaluate inter-coder reliability. Two annotators annotated them separately. Inter-coder agreement was then calculated using Cohen's Kappa. We first evaluate the agreement on whether a headline describes a health claim (see Table 1). The Cohen's Kappa for this annotation task is 0.71, indicating substantial agreement. The main disagreement is on headlines with non-verb words to express relations, such as *"behind"* in *"Identifying a genetic mutation behind sporadic Parkinson's disease"*, which was neglected occasionally.

| | | Annotator B | |
		No Health Claim	Health Claim
Annotator A	**No Health Claim**	14	9
	Health Claim	0	77

Table 1: Confusion matrix from whether a headline describe a relation.

We then compared inter-coder agreement on IV, DV, and relation annotations on the 77 headlines with health claims identified by both annotators. Since these annotations are text snippets rather than categories, we convert the original annotations to five categories: "IV", "DV", "Relation", "Multiple IVs" and "No Annotation", and then examine each text snippet that has been annotated by either annotator, assigning it to the annotator's chosen category. Since annotations from two annotators may not be totally the same, we consider two annotations are the same if they share the main keywords or phrases. For example, consider a headline *"Breast, ovarian cancer may have similar origins, study finds"*. One person annotated it as "IV-relation-DV" structure, *"Breast, ovarian cancer; may have; similar origins"* while the other annotated as "relation-Multiple IVs" structure, *"may have similar origins; Breast, ovarian cancer"*. The two annotations correspond to each other as "IV" vs. "Multiple IVs", "Relation" vs. "Relation" and "DV" vs. "Relation". The confusion matrix was then generated accordingly (Table 2), and Cohen's Kappa is 0.89.

There are mainly two types of disagreement on IV, DV, and relation annotations. One is how to distinguish "IV-relation-DV" and "relation-Multiple IVs" structures on headlines with multiple IVs or DVs, such as *"Breast, ovarian cancer may have similar origins, study finds"*. The other type of disagreements is whether a preposition phrase should be "DV" or not. For example, as for the headline *"A novel cancer immunotherapy shows early promise in preclinical studies"*, one annotator annotated *"preclinical studies"* as "DV", but the other thought *"preclinical studies"* an adverbial modifier of *"shows early promise in"* and no "DV" in that headline.

| | | Annotator B | | | | |
		IV	Relation	DV	Multiple IVs	No Annotation
	IV	68	3	2	2	2
	Relation	0	75	1	0	1
Annotator A	**DV**	0	2	71	1	3
	Multiple IVs	0	0	0	0	0
	No Annotation	0	0	0	0	0

Table 2: Confusion matrix from IV, DV and relation annotations.

3.4 The Annotated Dataset

After the inter-coder reliability check, the disagreements were resolved through discussion. Then one annotator annotated the remaining news headlines. Among the 564 headlines, 416 (74%) describe health claims and 148 (26%) do not. Each of the 416 headlines with health claims was annotated as one "IV-relation-DV" triplet with a few exceptions. Five headlines were annotated with "Multiple IVs" (e.g., "*Little to no association between butter consumption, chronic disease or total mortality*"); two described more than one "IV-relation-DV" triplet (e.g., "*Epigenetic modification increases susceptibility to obesity and predicts fatty liver*"). We have also identified six types of linguistic structures in health news headlines that might confuse the extractors:

- Non-verb relation: such as "*New potential treatment for cancer metastasis identified*".

- Relation with modal verb: such as "*Smoking can hamper common treatment for breast cancer*".

- IVs and DVs with prepositional phrases: such as "*Sugars in Western diets*" in "*Sugars in Western diets increase risk for breast cancer tumors and metastasis*".

- Multiple IVs or DVs in parallel phrases: parallel phrases mean to contain more than one IVs or DVs, such as "*breast, ovarian cancer*" in "*Breast, ovarian cancer may have similar origins, study finds*".

- Headlines containing both reporting verb and another verb to describe the relation: such as "*find*" and "*treat*" in "*Scientists find 'outlier' enzymes, potential new targets to treat diabetes, inflammation*".

- Headlines as incomplete sentences: such as "*Sugar-sweetened drinks linked to increased visceral fat*".

The 416 headlines with health claims include 113 with incomplete sentence structure (27%), 39 with reporting verbs (9%), 39 non-verb relations (9%), 108 with modal verbs (26%), 107 with prepositional phrases in IVs (26%), 182 with prepositional phrases in DVs (44%), 18 with parallel phrases in IVs (4%), 42 with parallel phrases in DVs (10%). One headline may include multiple characteristics.

As a robustness check, we further compared the linguistic characteristics of the headlines about two diseases: "breast cancer" and "diabetes", and found no significant difference (see Figure 1). Therefore, we consider the linguistic characteristics of health news headlines independent of disease types.

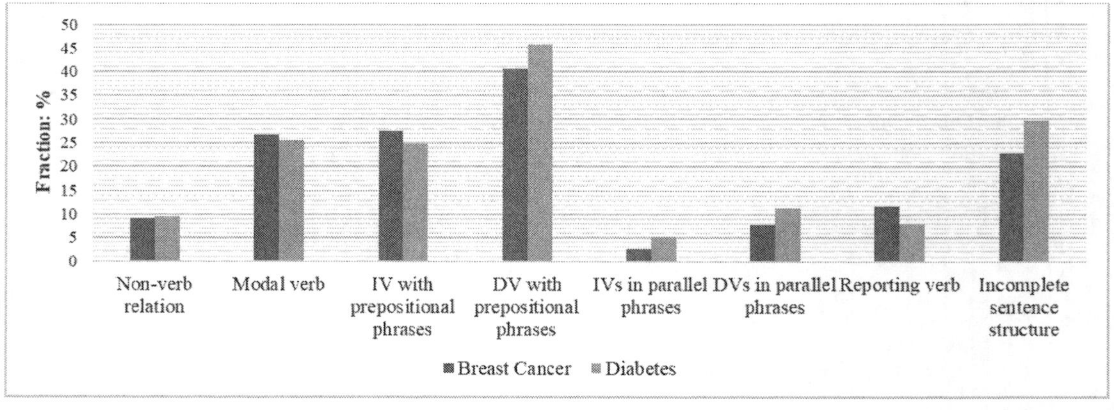

Figure 1: Distribution of different linguistic structures on breast cancer and diabetes.

4 Experiment Method and Result

Four systems were compared in terms of their performance in extracting "IV-relation-DV" from health news headlines. Section 4.1 describes the evaluation method. Section 4.2 evaluates performance on identifying headlines without health claims, and Section 4.3 on headlines with health claims. Section 4.4 evaluates performance on cases with special linguistic structures.

4.1 Evaluation Method

We chose two methods for this evaluation: the first one calculates the precision, recall and F-measure by manually comparing the machine annotations against the gold standard; the second method automatically calculates the BLEU scores between machine annotations and the gold standard.

Precision, Recall and F-measure are traditional evaluation methods in information retrieval. For information extraction task, Fader et al. (2011) and Etzioni et al. (2011) defined precision as the fraction of returned extractions that are correct, and recall as the fraction of correct extractions in the total corpus. For each extracted triplet, we manually check whether it is correct or not. The correct extraction is defined as keywords or phrases match in IV, DV and relation.

For robustness check we choose the second evaluation method as the BLEU score, which can be automatically calculated. As a popular measure in machine translation, it evaluates the similarity between the machine translations and the gold standard. The BLEU score divides each translated sentence into several n-grams and compares differences between a machine translation and a professional human translation based on those n-grams (Papineni et al., 2002).

In our task, we consider each manually-annotated "IV-relation-DV" triplet as a reference translation, and each machine-extracted triplet as a candidate translation. For each extractor, we will calculate a BLEU score. The higher BLEU score is, the better performance an extractor would achieve. The maximum number of n-grams varies from 2 to 4 and the weights for each n-gram are equal. In addition, we apply "Add-one Smoothing" technique proposed in Lin and Och (2004) to avoid the BLEU score being 0 when n grows bigger.

4.2 Headlines without Health Claim

In our benchmark data set, 26% headlines do not contain health claims. Correct extractions should return no triplets for such headlines. To evaluate the extractors on this task, we define precision as the correct results with no triplets among all results with no triplets, and recall as the correct results with no triplets among all headlines without claims. Table 3 shows the confusion matrix from each extractor and Table 4 shows the precision, recall and F-measure. The result shows that no extractors performed well in this task with all F-measures below 0.5 with little variation. Furthermore, OLLIE and OPENIE-5.0 had better precisions, but REVERB and SemRep had better recalls.

		Headlines without claims	Headlines with claims
REVERB	Results with no triplets	114	208
	Results with triplets	34	208
OLLIE		Headlines without claims	Headlines with claims
	Results with no triplets	77	107
	Results with triplets	71	309
OPENIE-5.0		Headlines without claims	Headlines with claims
	Results with no triplets	60	60
	Results with triplets	88	356
SemRep		Headlines without claims	Headlines with claims
	Results with no triplets	115	262
	Results with triplets	33	154

Table 3: Confusion matrix from different tools.

Information Extractor	Precision	Recall	F-measure
REVERB	.35	.77	**.48**
OLLIE	.42	.52	.46
OPENIE-5.0	**.50**	.41	.45
SemRep	.31	**.78**	.44

Table 4: Precision, Recall and F-measure for different tools on headlines without health claim.

An analysis of the false positive extractions shows that the main problem is the broad definition of relation in the three general-purpose tools, and thus many verbs that do not describe health claims were still identified as relations. For example, consider a news headline without health claim, *"New study explores concerns of African American breast cancer survivors"*, the triplet is *"New study; explores; concerns of African American breast cancer survivors"* from REVERB, OLLIE, OPENIE-5.0. In contrast, SemRep is stricter on the definition of relations, which results in higher recall, but at the same time low precision with many headlines with health claims not identified as well.

4.3 Headlines with Health Claim

In this section, we evaluate the extractors' performance on headlines with health claims. The manual evaluation (Table 5) shows that OPENIE-5.0 ranked highest in F-measure at .62, followed by OLLIE at .53, REVERB at .41 and SemRep at .13. In Table 6, OPENIE-5.0 also ranked highest in BLEU score, followed by REVERB and OLLIE, regardless of the maximum number of n-grams. Overall, OPENIE-5.0 is the best tool for extracting "IV-relation-DV" in headlines with health claims, leaving some room for improvement. The results also show that the SemRep, the tool dedicated to relation extraction in biomedical literature, does not generalize well to health news. In addition, REVERB and OLLIE achieved similar precision level to OPENIE-5.0, but their recalls are relatively lower.

Information Extractor	Precision	Recall	F-measure
REVERB	.61	.31	.41
OLLIE	.62	.46	.53
OPENIE-5.0	**.67**	**.57**	**.62**
SemRep	.23	.08	.13

Table 5: Precision, Recall and F-measure for different tools on headlines with health claim.

Information Extractor	BLEU Scores (N=2)	BLEU Scores (N=3)	BLEU Scores (N=4)
REVERB	.66	.66	.65
OLLIE	.61	.58	.54
OPENIE-5.0	**.74**	**.71**	**.69**
SemRep	.17	.13	.10

Table 6: BLEU scores for different tools on headlines with health claim.

Table 3 has shown the number of false negative extractions from all tools. SemRep has 262, the highest number, followed by REVERB, 208, OLLIE, 107, and OPENIE-5.0, 60. Among those headlines, 24 headlines are the most challenging, because none of the extractors was able to identify the triplets. 71% of them (17 out of 24) are incomplete sentences. Since OPENIE-5.0 is the best performing system, we examined the missing triplets in its output and found 58% (35 out of 60) are incomplete sentences. Therefore, incomplete sentences are particularly challenging for the extractors.

Our benchmark data set includes only five headlines with multiple IVs and two headlines with multiple relations. Because these are likely difficult cases, we particularly checked the extractors' performance on these headlines. For the five headlines annotated with "relation-Multiple IVs" structure, REVERB and SemRep both return no triplets. OPENIE-5.0 returns two triplets and OLLIE returns three, but none of those triplets were correct. For headlines with more than one "IV-relation-DV" triplets, OPEINIE-5.0 and REVERB return one correct triplet *"Epigenetic modification; predicts; fatty liver"* of *"Epigenetic modification increases susceptibility to obesity and predicts fatty liver"*, while others return no triplet or wrong triplets.

4.4 Impact of Linguistic Structures in Headlines

We then further examined the impact of the specific linguistic structures described in Section 3.4 on individual extractors (Table 7). If ranking the task difficulty by the best F-measure for each linguistic type, identifying non-verb relation is the most challenging with best F-measure at 0.19 by SemRep. Second, identifying triplets in incomplete sentences is also challenging with best F-measure at 0.30 by OLLIE and 0.28 by OPENIE-5.0. The extractors performed slightly better on two tasks with best F-measure at 0.40 level: identifying multiple IVs or DVs in parallel phrases, and identifying actual verb relations when reporting verbs are used. The extractors performed best on the tasks of identify-ing verb relations (including modal verbs) and identifying prepositional phrases in IVs and DVs with best F-measures over 0.6.

Structure Type	Information Extractor	Precision	Recall	F-measure
Non-verb Relation	REVERB	0	0	0
	OLLIE	.10	.05	.07
	OPENIE-5.0	0	0	0
	SemRep	**.33**	**.13**	**.19**
Verb Relation	REVERB	.64	.34	.44
	OLLIE	.66	.50	.57
	OPENIE-5.0	**.71**	**.63**	**.67**
	SemRep	.22	.08	.12
Modal Verb	REVERB	.70	.48	.57
	OLLIE	.76	.65	.70
	OPENIE-5.0	**.88**	**.88**	**.88**
	SemRep	.34	.11	.17
Prepositional Phrase in IV	REVERB	.35	.18	.24
	OLLIE	.57	.46	.51
	OPENIE-5.0	**.65**	**.57**	**.61**
	SemRep	.10	.05	.06
Prepositional Phrase in DV	REVERB	.67	.35	.46
	OLLIE	.68	.55	.61
	OPENIE-5.0	**.72**	**.63**	**.67**
	SemRep	.19	.10	.13
Parallel phrases for Multiple IVs	REVERB	.25	.06	.09
	OLLIE	.29	.22	.25
	OPENIE-5.0	**.40**	**.33**	**.36**
	SemRep	.11	.06	.07
Parallel phrases for Multiple DVs	REVERB	.67	.19	.30
	OLLIE	.41	.31	.35
	OPENIE-5.0	**.46**	**.41**	**.43**
	SemRep	.16	.07	.10
Headlines with Reporting Verbs	REVERB	.36	.23	.28
	OLLIE	.23	.18	.20
	OPENIE-5.0	**.41**	**.38**	**.39**
	SemRep	.29	.10	.15
Incomplete Sentences	REVERB	.50	.09	.15
	OLLIE	**.40**	**.24**	**.30**
	OPENIE-5.0	.35	.24	.28
	SemRep	.29	.11	.16

Table 7: Performance on different linguistic structures.

5 Challenges to Individual Extractors

Based on the above results, we summarize the main challenges for each extractor and offer suggestions for improvement.

SemRep: SemRep outputs significantly fewer triplets than the other tools. It even missed the cases with clear verb structures, such as *"Smoking can hamper common treatment for breast cancer"*. The restriction may be attributed to SemRep's strict definition on some entities and relations. For example, "associated with" is defined as the relation between a gene and a disease only (Kilicoglu et al., 2011). Therefore, loosening the definition on some entities and relations might be helpful.

REVERB: Since REVERB is a verb-based extractor, the first suggestion is to add some rules for processing headlines with non-verb relations. In addition, the ability to recognizing IV and DV in complicated noun phrases should also be improved. In such cases, REVERB missed the head nouns in complicated noun phrases. For example, the IV extracted by REVERB is *"humans"* in healine *"One of the most common viruses in humans may promote breast cancer development"*.

OLLIE: Headlines with reporting verb bring a big problem to OLLIE. OLLIE tends to extract the reporting verbs as the relations while ignore the actual verb relations. For example, for the headline *"Scientists find 'outlier' enzymes, potential new targets to treat diabetes, inflammation"*, OLLIE identified *"Scientists; find; 'outlier' enzymes"* as the triplet, but missed the actual health claim that the enzymes may be able to treat diabetes.

OPENIE-5.0: OPENIE-5.0 faces the challenges of non-verb relations and incomplete sentences. Especially, for headlines with "A linked to B" structure, OPENIE-5.0 can only identify triplets without DVs. For example, OPENIE-5.0 identified *"Sugar-sweetened drinks; linked;"* in *"Sugar-sweetened drinks linked to increased visceral fat"*.

6 Conclusion

In this paper, we have created a benchmark data set, and used both manual and automated evaluation methods to compare the performance of four information extractors on identifying the health claims in health news headlines. Both methods reached consistent findings. Overall, 26% of health news headlines do not include health claims, and 74% do. The three general-purpose extractors (OPENIE-5.0, OLLIE, REVERB) performed better than the biomedicine-specific extractor (SemRep), probably because SemRep was developed for documents in academic writing, not popular science writing. Among those general-purpose extractors, OPENIE-5.0 has the best performance to extract "IV-relation-DV" triplets with F-measure at 0.6 level. However, some characteristic linguistic structures in health news headlines pose particular challenge to these extractors, especially on identifying non-verb relations and relations in incomplete sentences. With F-measure at 0.4 level, further improvement is needed for identifying multiple IVs or DVs in parallel phrases, or identifying actual verb relations when reporting verbs are around. The extractors can identify verb relations and prepositional phrases in IVs and DVs relatively well with F-measure at 0.6 level. In future work, we would like to develop new tools for identifying headlines without claims and enrich the current rule-based systems with rules tailored to the linguistic characteristics of health news headlines.

Acknowledgements

We would like to thank Dr. Jun Wang for providing the data. This research was partially supported by China Scholarship Council and Syracuse University.

References

Michele Banko, Michael J Cafarella, Stephen Soderland, Matt Broadhead and Oren Etzioni. 2007. *Open information extraction from the web.* In IJCAI (Vol. 7, pp. 2670-2676).

Mollyann Brodie, Elizabeth C. Hamel, Drew E. Altman, Robert J. Blendon and John M. Benson. 2003. *Health news and the American public, 19962002.* Journal of Health Politics, Policy and Law, 28(5), 927-950.

Janara Christensen, Mausam, Stephen Soderland, and Oren Etzioni. 2011. *An Analysis of Open Information Extraction Based on Semantic Role Labeling.* In Proceedings of the Sixth International Conference on Knowledge Capture (pp. 113120). New York, NY, USA: ACM.

Lipika Dey, Muhammad Abulaish, Jahiruddin and Gaurav Sharma. 2007. *Text Mining through Entity-Relationship Based Information Extraction.* In 2007 IEEE/WIC/ACM International Conferences on Web Intelligence and Intelligent Agent Technology - Workshops (pp. 177180).

Oren Etzioni, Anthony Fader, Janara Christensen, Stephen Soderland, and Mausam. 2011. *Open Information Extraction: The Second Generation.* In IJCAI (Vol. 11, pp. 3-10)

Anthony Fader, Stephen Soderland, and Oren Etzioni. 2011. *Identifying Relations for Open Information Extraction.* In Proceedings of the Conference on Empirical Methods in Natural Language Processing (pp. 15351545). Stroudsburg, PA, USA: Association for Computational Linguistics.

FDA. 2009. *Guidance Documents & Regulatory Information by Topic - Guidance for Industry: Evidence-Based Review System for the Scientific Evaluation of Health Claims.* `https://www.fda.gov/Food/GuidanceRegulation/GuidanceDocumentsRegulatoryInformation/ucm073332.htm` (last access: May 10, 2018)

Boris Katz and Jimmy Lin. 2000. *REXTOR: A System for Generating Relations from Natural Language.* In ACL-2000 Workshop on Recent Advances in Natural Language Processing and Information Retrieval (pp. 6777). Hong Kong, China: Association for Computational Linguistics.

Halil Kilicoglu, Graciela Rosemblat, Marcelo Fiszman and Thomas C Rindflesch. 2011. *Constructing a semantic predication gold standard from the biomedical literature.* BMC Bioinformatics, 12, 486.

Chin-Yew Lin and Franz Josef Och. 2004. *Automatic Evaluation of Machine Translation Quality Using Longest Common Subsequence and Skip-bigram Statistics.* In Proceedings of the 42Nd Annual Meeting on Association for Computational Linguistics. Stroudsburg, PA, USA: Association for Computational Linguistics.

Mausam. 2016. *Open information extraction systems and downstream applications.* In Proceedings of the Twenty-Fifth International Joint Conference on Artificial Intelligence (pp. 4074-4077). AAAI Press.

Mausam, Michael Schmitz, Robert Bart, Stephen Soderland, and Oren Etzioni. 2012. *Open Language Learning for Information Extraction.* In Proceedings of the 2012 Joint Conference on Empirical Meth-ods in Natural Language Processing and Computational Natural Language Learning (pp. 523534). Stroudsburg, PA, USA: Association for Computational Linguistics.

NPR. 2018. *How to make great headlines.* `http://training.npr.org/digital/the-checklist-for-writing-good-headlines/` (last visited May 14th, 2018)

Harinder Pal and Mausam. 2016. *Demonyms and Compound Relational Nouns in Nominal Open IE.* In Proceedings of the 5th Workshop on Automated Knowledge Base Construction (pp. 3539). San Diego, CA: Association for Computational Linguistics.

Kishore Papineni, Salim Roukos, Todd Ward, and Wei-Jing Zhu. 2002. *BLEU: A Method for Automatic Evaluation of Machine Translation.* In Proceedings of the 40th Annual Meeting on Association for Computational Linguistics (pp. 311318). Stroudsburg, PA, USA: Association for Computational Linguistics.

Thomas C. Rindflesch and Marcelo Fiszman. 2003. *The interaction of domain knowledge and linguistic structure in natural language processing: interpreting hypernymic propositions in biomedical text.* Journal of Biomedical Informatics, 36(6), 462477.

Mary-Anne Saari, Candace Gibson and Andrew Osler. 1998. *Endangered species: science writers in the Canadian daily press.* Public Understanding of Science, 7(1), 61-81.

Swarnadeep Saha, Harinder Pal and Mausam. 2017. *Bootstrapping for Numerical Open IE.* In Proceedings of the 55th Annual Meeting of the Association for Computational Linguistics (Volume 2: Short Papers) (pp. 317323). Vancouver, Canada: Association for Computational Linguistics.

Petroc Sumner, Solveiga Vivian-Griffiths, Jacky Boivin, Andy Williams, Christos A Venetis, Aime Davies, Jack Ogden, Leanne Whelan, Bethan Hughes, Bethan Dalton, Fred Boy and Christopher D Chambers. 2014. *The association between exaggeration in health related science news and academic press releas-es: retrospective observational study.* BMJ, 349, g7015.

Melinda Voss. 2002. *Checking the Pulse: Midwestern Reporters' Opinions on Their Ability to Report Health Care News.* American Journal of Public Health, 92(7), 11581160.

Fei Wu and Daniel S. Weld. 2010. *Open Information Extraction Using Wikipedia.* In Proceedings of the 48th Annual Meeting of the Association for Computational Linguistics (pp. 118127). Stroudsburg, PA, USA: Association for Computational Linguistics.

Crowdsourcing StoryLines:
Harnessing the Crowd for Causal Relation Annotation

Tommaso Caselli
RUG / Groningen, NL
t.caselli@rug.nl

Oana Inel
VU / Amsterdam, NL
oana.inel@vu.nl

Abstract

This paper describes a crowdsourcing experiment on the annotation of plot-like structures in English news articles. The CrowdTruth methodology and metrics have been applied to select valid annotations from the crowd. We further run an in-depth analysis of the annotated data by comparing it with available expert data. Our results show a valuable use of crowdsourcing annotations for such complex semantic tasks, and promote a new annotation approach that combines crowd and experts.

1 Introduction

Causal relations are a pervasive phenomenon in human activities, including narrative production. Causality is actually the main component of narratives, regardless of the mediums (novels, news articles, comments, micro-blogs, pictures, among others) and their fictional status (fictional vs. non-fictional narratives). In a narrative text, causal connections between events allow the story to progress, the actors to participate, and eventually reach a conclusion. Causality is responsible for logically connecting the events together in a meaningful way.

If we shift perspective, and look at narratives from the point of view of the producers rather than their structural properties, it is easy to observe how humans impose causal, or explanatory, relations among events that they perceive or are involved into. Humans have a great appetite for information and are in constant need to find explanations for the things they observe. We search the present for cues and evidence, merge and resolve information with what we already known (i.e., the past), and use this information to (try to) predict the future and make decisions. Explanatory relations and narrative strategies are one of the major cognitive tools we use to observe the world and, most importantly, to interpret it (Boyd, 2009; Gottschall, 2012). When reporting on an event in the world, or telling someone a personal experience, we do not merely describe what happens, i.e., we do not just list events in the order of occurrence [1], but we connect them in a set of coherent patterns, or, in other words, we give rise to *plot structures* (Bal, 1997). Plot structures express a form of reasoning about causal relations between events and states composing the narrative (Lehnert, 1981; Goyal et al., 2010; Mani, 2012).

The current stream of data and information is growing everyday and its size and complexity is such that humans may suffer from "information overload". To minimise such a problem, intelligent content management systems have been developed and they became more and more popular and used. Different methods and approaches have been developed to provide users with personalised and relevant information. However, most of this information is given in the form of full text documents that require the users to read them to identify (i.e., extract) the information. Automatic processing would be beneficial, especially if the results are presented as structured data based on narrative strategies. We follow, in this

---

[1]For a comparison, think about the Ancient Roman tradition of the *Annales*, concise historical records merely reporting events chronologically.

Proceedings of the Workshop on Events and Stories in the News, pages 44–54
Santa Fe, New Mexico, USA, August 20, 2018.

respect, the proposal of automatically generating storylines of events (Vossen et al., 2015; Caselli and Vossen, 2016).

This paper reports on a crowdsourcing experiment on the annotation of causal relations between pairs of events in news data.

The main contributions of this work are:

- an analysis of the crowdsourced data, in terms of parameters that may affect the annotation quality, time, and evaluation of the data using the CrowdTruth methodology (Aroyo and Welty, 2014; Aroyo and Welty, 2015);

- a comparison between experts and crowdsourced annotated data with respect to a publicly available reference benchmark corpus for storyline evaluation, the Event StoryLine Corpus (ESC) (Caselli and Vossen, 2017);

- the release of an enhanced version of the Event Storyline Corpus (ESC v1.2).

The remainder of the paper is organised as follows: Section 2 provides an overview of related work on the annotation of causal relations in different datasets, highlighting differences and commonalities with our contribution. Section 3 describes the dataset and the crowdsourcing experiment settings based on the CrowdTruth metrics. Section 4 reports on an in-depth analysis of the crowd data and its comparison with existing expert annotated data. Finally, Section 5 summarises our findings and suggests directions for future work.

2   Related Work

Causality can be broadly defined as the knowledge, or way of knowing, if an event, or a state of affairs, is responsible for *causing* another one. To avoid the intrinsic circularity of this definition, we can rephrase it in more generic terms such that causality establishes a connection between two processes, events, or states, whereby the first is (partly) responsible for the occurrence, or holding as true, of the second, and the second is (partly) dependent on the first.

Causality has been subject of debates in different scientific communities. One of the most relevant aspect of this debate is the lack of a homogeneous theory of causality, and, most importantly, the availability of a plurality of perspectives on it. Providing an extensive and critical summary of this debate is out of the scope of this work, but, we will review relevant works in the areas of Linguistics and Natural Language Processing that contributed to shape this notion, its annotation in actual natural language data, and the development of automatic systems. We restrict this literature review to approaches in the news domain.

One of the distinguishing properties of causality in natural language, shared with other semantic relations such as meronymy and mereology, is granularity (Hobbs, 1985; Mulkar-Mehta et al., 2011). This allows humans to interactively play between coarse-grained and fine-grained levels of causality. Further studies (Talmy, 1976; Comrie, 1981; Girju and Moldovan, 2002) have investigated the variety of lexico and semantic constructions that can express causation in a natural language. At least for English, as well as other Indo-European languages, it is possible to differentiate the set of causative constructions into two big groups: i.) those expressing causality via **explicit** patterns; and ii.) those using **implicit** patterns. The difference between these two ways of expressing causality relies in the semantic transparency of the causative constructions. Explicit causative constructions are characterised by the presence of keywords such as causal connectives, adverbs or adjectives (e.g. *because (of)*, *with the results that, since, so*), causation verbs (e.g. *cause, bring about, kill, blacken*), and conditional constructions, among others. On the other hand, implicit causation can be expressed by complex nominals (e.g. $malaria_{NP1}$ $mosquitoes_{NP2}$, where NP2 is interpreted as causing NP1 [2]), verbs of implicit causation, and discourse structure.

The annotation of expressions of causality, or causal language, has received lots of attention which resulted in the realisation of different annotation schemes and initiatives. Computational lexicons, such

---

[2]This example is extracted from (Girju and Moldovan, 2002).

as WordNet (Miller, 1995), VerbNet (Schuler, 2005), PropBank (Kingsbury and Palmer, 2002), and FrameNet (Baker et al., 1998), were the first to encode this information at the level of lexical items or senses. For instance, WordNet encodes two relations, such as *causes* and *entailments*. VerbNet and PropBank include causative verbs. FrameNet represents causality through a variety of frames (e.g. CAUSATION, THWARTING) and roles (e.g. PURPOSE).

The Penn Discourse Treebank (PDTB) (Prasad et al., 2007) models causality as inference of discourse relations. Causality is a subclass of the contingency relation hierarchy, together with enablement and condition. The definition of causality we have used in the crowdsourcing experiments is strictly connected to that of contingency of the PDTB. However, we annotate relations between pairs of events rather than between discourse units.

Other initiatives concern three different annotation projects: CaTeRS (Mostafazadeh et al., 2016b), CATENA (Mirza and Tonelli, 2016), and BeCauSE 2.0 (Dunietz et al., 2017). The first two projects, based on the TimeML annotation scheme (Pustejovsky et al., 2003), annotate causality between pairs of events. CaTeRs adopts a commonsense reasoning perspective, rather than limiting the annotation to the presence of specific linguistic markers. The scheme adopts three values (`cause`, `enable`, and `prevent` (Wolff, 2007)) to be annotated as "true" with respect to the actual context of occurrence of the event pairs. The authors report a global Fleiss's κ score on all annotated relations (including also temporal relations) of $\kappa = 0.49$ without closure, and $\kappa = 0.51$ with closure. CATENA adopts a linguistic approach. The annotation of a causal relation is allowed only between pairs of events *in presence of* a non-discontinuous causal connective, i.e., limited to explicit relations. Finally, BeCauSE still addresses the annotation in terms of a linguistic approach, requiring the presence of a causal connective for the annotation to take place. The main difference with respect to CATENA and other initiatives concerns the fact that it annotates all constructions that express causality rather than restricting to a particular realisation (e.g. discourse relations, or TimeML events). The approach we have adopted in our crowdsourcing experiments follows CaTeRs as we have adopted a commonsense reasoning perspective. However, we have simplified the granularity of the values to one type only, cause, finding the three-way classification too fine grained for the crowd.

Other works have addressed causality in the broader context of automatically learning narrative structures, or plot-like structures, using unsupervised methods. A notable work in this area is the Narrative Event Chains (Chambers and Jurafsky, 2008). Narrative chains are partially ordered sequences of events related to a common protagonist, i.e., sequences of verbs sharing a common actor, identified through typed dependencies, obtained from a large corpus collection. Narrative chains do not model causality directly, but they assume that narratives, such as news articles, are coherent structures. This means that if a sequence of verbs shares a coreferring argument, then these verbs must be connected by the discourse structure. One of the main criticism of this approach is that the chains express more co-occurrence relations rather than actual narrative relations, and, in some cases, may result in non-coherent chains of events.

Crowdsourcing of causal relations has received less attention than other natural language processing tasks, such as event extraction and factuality assessment (Lee et al., 2015), temporal information extraction (Caselli et al., 2016; Snow et al., 2008), word sense disambiguation (Jurgens, 2013; Akkaya et al., 2010), among others. To study narratives, (Hu and Broniatowski, 2017) proposed a crowdsourcing approach to represent a text, which is split into smaller text snippets, as a causal network. The crowd workers were asked to draw links between text snippets that are related through a causal relation, in an external tool. In a similar way, creative writing crowdsourcing tasks have been developed (Mostafazadeh et al., 2016a) to build a corpus of commonsense stories containing causal and temporal relations between everyday events. Other initiatives have annotated causal relations between propositions (Sukhareva et al., 2016), among other context-sensitive semantic verb relations, i.e., co-reference, temporal, entailment. The crowd workers had an observed agreement of 71.8%, where Krippendorff's α was equal to 0.32 on a very limited set (i.e., there were only between 2%-6% of causal relations in the entire dataset). In this work, we specifically focus on identifying loose causal relations between events in a large variety of topics using simplified crowdsourcing instructions.

3 Crowdsourcing Causal Relations between Events

As already stated, we follow a commonsense reasoning approach to annotate causality. Furthermore, our goal is to approximate the annotation of plot-like structures rather than strict causal relations between pairs of linguistic items. In the rest of the paper, we use causal relations and plot-like relations as synonym terms. Thus, causality is naively used to refer to the broader notion of contingent relations. This choice is also dictated by a desire to be as much ecological as possible with respect to the crowd in the process of data collection. In our vision, ecology is declined in two ways: i.) avoid to bias the crowd with lengthy and complex task instructions (including examples); ii.) collect a diversity of judgements assuming multi-faceted versions of ground truth data, i.e., there is no such a thing as absolute right or wrong, but varieties of truths. In the remainder of this section, we describe the dataset (Section 3.1), the crowdsourcing annotation template (Section 3.2), the quality metrics used to evaluate the crowdsourced data (Section 3.3) and the crowdsourcing experiments performed (Section 3.4). The data and the crowd annotations are publicly available. [3]

3.1 Dataset

The experimental dataset covers 22 topics from the Event StoryLine Corpus v1.0 (ESC v1.0) (Caselli and Vossen, 2017). The ESC corpus contains expert annotations that cover a high range of entities and relations such as: actors, locations, temporal expressions, events, temporal relations, event coreference relations, and plot-like relations between pairs of events. The plot relations in the ESC data are marked with a <PLOT_LINK> tag, and broadly correspond to contingent relations between pairs of events. The annotation of these links is based on relatively simple annotation guidelines, instructing the annotators in the identification of the eligible pairs of events and associated relation (i.e., relation directionality). The inter-annotator agreement for <PLOT_LINK> has been calculated using the Dice coefficient and equals 0.638.

ESC consists of 22 topics, for a total of 281 news articles. We extracted 1,204 annotated sentences containing at least two expert annotated events. Following the approach of the ESC corpus, we have excluded events belonging to the following classes from the event pairs: ASPECTUAL, REPORTING, CAUSATIVE, and GENERIC. These classes actually represent sets of event mentions which cannot give rise to a plot-like structure, or a contingent relation. For instance, on the one hand, in the case of a REPORTING event (e.g. *say*, *report*), a plot-like relation holds with respect to the actual content of what is "reported" rather than between the marker of the presence of a reporting event. On the other hand, CAUSATIVE events (e.g. *cause*, *sparkle*, *trigger*) have been excluded as they are interpreted as explicit markers of a causal relation. The actual plot relation holds between their arguments. An overview of the dataset is shown in Table 1. The ESC dataset contains 2,290 manually annotated <PLOT_LINK> relations between event pairs. This set of relations is then expanded to 5,684 pairs when using coreference relations. As for the manually annotated pairs, only 1,571 out of 2,290 (68.6%) occur in the same sentence. In the 1,204 sentences that we selected in our experiments, there are only 1,540 expert annotated event pairs, that are further used in our analysis (Section 4).

Table 1: Dataset Overview

#Topics	#Doc	#Sent	#Event Pairs	# Expert Annotation ESC v1.0	# Expert Pairs ESC v1.0 in Our Experiments
22	281	1,204	7,778	1,571	1,540

3.2 Crowdsourcing Annotation Template

We ran the crowdsourcing experiments on the Figure Eight[4] platform, formerly known as CrowdFlower. Figure 1 shows the annotation template used to gather crowd annotations on causal relations between

---

event pairs. The annotation template uses simplified instructions that can all be seen in Figure 1, i.e., we did not provide detailed instructions or annotation guidelines, nor examples. In short, the workers were given a sentence and a list of expressions to validate. An expression consists of one of the statements $Event_A$ causes $Event_B$ or $Event_A$ is caused by $Event_B$, where $Event_A$ (E_A) and $Event_B$ (E_B) appear in the sentence. For example, the sentence shown in Figure 1 contains three events: *warns*, *bombs* and *war*. Taking all possible combinations of these three events, the crowd is asked to validate the following expressions: *warns* causes *bombs*, *warns* is caused by *bombs*, *warns* causes *war*, *warns* is caused by *war*, *bombs* causes *war*, *bombs* is caused by *war*. To help workers identify the position of the two events composing each expression in the sentence, the events are highlighted in the sentence when hovering over the given expression. For instance, in Figure 1 we hover over the expression *warns* is caused by *bombs* (grey background), and therefore, the events *warns* and *bombs* are highlighted in blue in the sentence. The workers were allowed to choose as many expressions as they considered valid. In case no valid expression was found for the given sentence, the crowd workers were asked to motivate their answer in a text field.

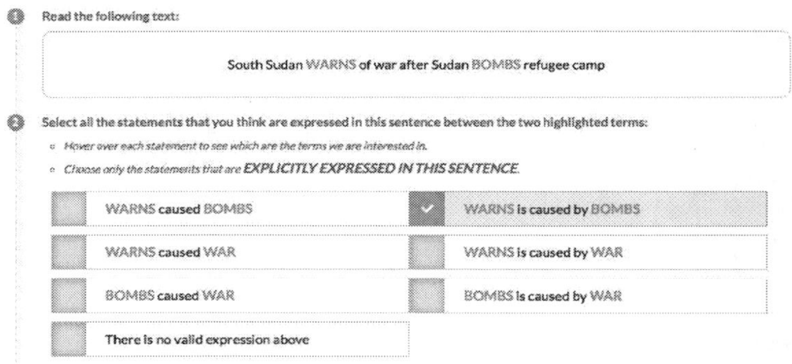

Figure 1: Screenshot of the Crowdsourcing Template to Annotate Causal Relations between Events.

3.3   Crowdsourcing Quality Metrics

The task of extracting causal relations between events is prone to disagreement, diverse perspectives, and interpretations due to: i.) the inherent ambiguity of natural language; and ii.) the difficult nature of dealing with events and causality. To address and consider these aspects, we chose to evaluate the quality of the crowdsourced data by using the assumption behind the CrowdTruth disagreement-aware methodology (Aroyo and Welty, 2014; Aroyo and Welty, 2015): ambiguity is reflected in all crowdsourcing components (i.e., units, workers, annotations) and the ambiguity of each component influences the other components. For our usecase, a unit represents a sentence, the workers are the contributors from the Figure Eight platform, and the annotations are statements of type E_A causes/is caused by E_B, where E_A and E_B appear in the sentence, and the value *"NONE"*, from which the workers can choose, as described in Section 3.2. A worker judgement is composed of such validated statements.

In this work, we followed and applied the CrowdTruth methodology and metrics as suggested in (Dumitrache et al., 2018). For our use case, the identification of causal relations between events, each worker's judgement is translated into a binary worker vector, $WorkerVec$, which has a length equal to $n{+}1$, where n is the total number of causal relation statements to choose from and the last component refers to the value *"NONE"*. Each causal relation component that was picked by the worker gets a value of 1, and 0 otherwise. The $WorkerVec$ of all workers that annotated the same sentence s are summed up to compute the sentence vector, $SentVec$. These two vectors are then used to compute the quality score for each sentence, worker and causal relation, in particular:

- *unit quality score* (UQS): represents the degree of agreement among the workers that annotated the sentence s, i.e., the lower the score, the less clear the sentence. UQS is computed as the average cosine similarity between all $WorkerVec$ for s, weighted by the worker quality (WQS).

- *worker quality* (WQS): represents the degree of a worker's agreement with the rest of the workers on the specific task. WQS of worker i is computed as the product of 2 cosine similarity metrics - the worker-worker agreement WWA (a pair-wise agreement between every two workers) and the worker-sentence agreement WSA (the agreement of a worker with all the workers that annotated the same sentence); the two worker metrics are weighted by the unit quality score UQS; thus, the annotations of the workers with lower quality score will weight less in the final output.

- *sentence - causal relation score* ($SCausalRel$): represents the likelihood of the causal relation r to be expressed in sentence s. $SCausalRel$ is computed as the ratio of the number of workers that picked the causal relation r over all workers that annotated the sentence, weighted by WQS.

Using these preliminaries, the CrowdTruth metrics model the inter-dependency between the three main components of the crowdsourcing experiments - units (sentences), workers and causal relation statements. The aforementioned quality metrics are computed in a dynamic fashion, iteratively, until the results are stable. As a result of this process, the final crowd annotations, the $SCausalRel$, are weighted by the quality of the workers that annotated the given unit. The reason for choosing the CrowdTruth approach to weight the annotations of the workers rather than those provided by the platform (in our case Figure Eight) is that the trust values of the crowdsourcing platform does not account for the ambiguity of the data that is annotated.

3.4 Crowdsourcing Data Collection

In total, we ran two crowdsourcing experiments, as show in Table 2 - a pilot experiment $TrialEventPairs$ on 4 topics and a main experiment $6EventPairs$ on all 22 topics. We ran the pilot experiment, $TrialEventPairs$, to identify the optimal settings in terms of number of event pairs to be shown at the same time to the workers. Figure 2 shows the distribution of UQS for each set of sentences containing between [1, 28] event pairs. Besides the distribution of UQS, the plot also shows the mean UQS value, the median UQS value and the number of sentences containing the given number of event pairs. There is a clear pattern between the increase of event pairs (X axis) and the decrease of the UQS. This suggests that the amount of event pairs influences the overall quality of the sentences and consequently, the performance of the workers on identifying causal relations between events. Given that for sentences containing more than 6 event pairs the mean UQS drops below 0.4 in most cases, we identified 6 event pairs as the optimal number. Therefore, in the main experiment ($6EventPairs$), the crowd needs to validate a maximum of 12 causal relation statements (2 for each pair of events).

Each unit, which is composed of a sentence and a set of causal relation statements, was annotated by 15 workers and each annotation was paid 2¢. The workers were categorized as level 2 according to Figure Eight, i.e., a smaller group of more experienced, higher accuracy contributors. For the $TrialEventPairs$ experiment we gathered 3,360 annotations from a total of 157 unique workers and for the $6EventPairs$ experiment we gathered 27,675 annotations from a total of 697 unique workers. We split our input units in batches of around 50 units, i.e., we were publishing jobs of around 50 units at a time. In each job, the workers were allowed to annotate as many units as they wanted, with a maximum limit of 20 units per job. In total, in the $TrailEventPairs$ experiment the workers annotated between 1 and 75 units, with an average of 21 units per worker and in the $6EventPairs$ experiments, the workers annotated between 1 and 457 units, with an average of 40 units per worker. The total cost of the two experiments was 756\$.

4 A Comparison with Experts

We ran a set of comparative analyses between the data collected through this crowdsourcing experiment and the annotations of <PLOT_LINK> in the ESC v1.0 dataset. Given that the CrowdTruth metrics allow us to estimate the quality of the annotated data, expressed by the *SCausalRel* score, we can use the different thresholds as corresponding to different qualities of the crowd annotated data. The usefulness of a comparison with expert data is in this case two-folded: i.) it provides additional evaluation of the crowd data which complements the CrowdTruth measures; ii.) it allows us to gain more insights on the

Table 2: Overview of crowdsourcing experiments to derive optimal annotation settings and template

Type	Exp.	Input Data				Crowdsourcing Template	
		#Topics	#Sent.	#Units	#Event Pairs	Annotations	Max # of Annotations
Pilot	*TrialEventPairs*	4	217	224	1,477	E_A causes E_B E_A caused by E_B NONE	57
Main	*6EventPairs*	22	1,204	1,845	7,778	E_A causes E_B E_A caused by E_B NONE	13

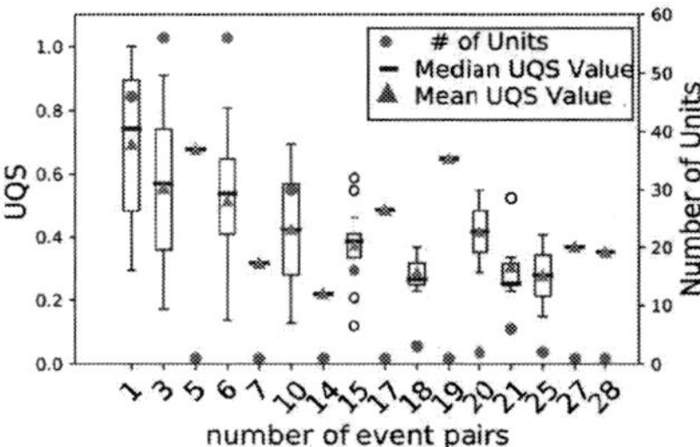

Figure 2: Distribution of UQS for any number of event pairs in the $TrialEventPairs$ pilot experiment.

differences between experts and crowd (in annotation behaviour), and to identify a reliability threshold for directly using the crowdsourced data as Gold Standard, or for integrating them with expert data.

The analysis was conducted as follows: first, we excluded all units that were marked as "*NONE*", regardless of the *SCausalRel* score. This allows us to access a large set of events pairs. In case there is actually no relation among the pairs, the *SCausalRel* score will be either very low or equal to zero, if no worker has annotated it. The *SCausalRel* score ranges between 0 and 1, where 1 expresses perfect agreement among all crowd annotators. After this, we have generated different thresholds, starting from 1 and lowering the score by a 0.1 point at a time, up to 0.5, a value signalling a 50% agreement among all workers. In this way, we can compare crowd data of different agreement with the expert data. We have used standard Precision (P), Recall (R), and F1-score (F1), assuming the expert data as a Gold Standard.

Table 3: Comparing Experts and Crowd: Causal Relation Identification

Threshold	P	R	F1	# Crowd Relations
1.0	0.923	0.007	0.015	13
0.9	0.764	0.086	0.155	174
0.8	0.670	0.191	0.297	440
0.7	0.547	0.298	0.386	838
0.6	0.424	0.424	0.424	1,540
0.5	0.316	0.546	0.401	2,654

Table 3 illustrates the results of the overall evaluation, i.e., the ability of the crowd to identify both the event pairs that stand in a causal relation and the directionality of the causal relation. As the figures show, there is a clear pattern: the lower the threshold, the higher the number of relations annotated by the crowd. Lower thresholds actually correspond to higher disagreement among the workers, pointing out differences in the interpretation of the sentences, as well as signalling the complexity of the task. In this case, the differences may concern the actual pair, the relation directionality, or both. We can also observe that lower thresholds correspond to an improvement of Recall (i.e. higher matching with experts), at the

Table 4: Comparing Experts and Crowd: Event Pairs Detection (only)

Threshold	P	R	F1	# Crowd Pairs	# FPs	# Unique FPs	%Correct FP
1.0	0.923	0.007	0.015	13	1	1	100%
0.9	0.787	0.088	0.159	174	37	36	77.77%
0.8	0.695	0.198	0.309	440	134	97	82.75%
0.7	0.586	0.314	0.409	827	342	208	63.38 %
0.6	0.480	0.453	0.466	1,456	757	415	56.41%
0.5	0.390	0.589	0.469	2,328	1,420	663	49.65%

cost of Precision. However, this level of analysis is too coarse grained. For instance, at a 0.6 *SCausalRel* score threshold, Precision and Recall are the same, and both of them are below 50%. On the one hand, this signals that the diversity (of the crowd) is valuable in identifying more relations than the experts. On the other hand, it does not tell us much about the quality of the data. We basically know that 60% of the times, the workers agree on the presence of a relation, and that they have identified much more relations than the experts. Although this is in line with our annotation approach based on commonsense reasoning (people, with diverse personal experiences, identify a larger set of likely relations), we do not know if the extra relations with respect to the experts are valid or not.

We thus conducted two additional analyses on the crowd data by inspecting, separately, the event pairs alone, and then, the relation directionality. This provides a better assessment of the quality of the crowd data as well as which sub-task is harder: the event pair identification or the relation directionality.

Table 4 reports on the results for the event pairs identification subtask. The mismatch between the number of crowd relations in Table 3 and that of the crowd pairs in Table 4 is due to the fact that in some cases both directionality values (i.e. causes and is caused by) have the same *SCausalRel*, or the *SCausalRel* is in the same threshold range, thus increasing the number of relations, especially for lower thresholds. The values for P, R and F1 are in line with those of the global evaluation (see Table 3). In this case, we have extended the analysis by manually inspecting 20% of the False Positives for each threshold, with the exclusion of threshold 1.0. The analysis shows that, until a threshold of 0.6, the majority of False Positives are actually valid pairs that were missed by the experts. As lower thresholds subsume all pairs from higher ones, the manual validation of the False Positives shows that it is possible to identify an optimal threshold for the crowd data, that in this case corresponds to 0.7, where 63.38% of the event pairs are actually valid. We have also analysed the non-valid cases. We have identified two reasons for the errors: i.) either the event pair is not valid in the actual context of occurrence (see example 1); or ii.) the event pair is genuinely wrong (see example 2).

1. *A powerful earthquake [...], **killing** at least five people and injuring dozens in a region devastated by the **quake**-triggered tsunami of 2004.* [ESC v1.0, 37_1, sentence 3]

2. *During the escape, Arcade Joseph Comeaux , Jr . [...] took them hostage and forced them to **drive** to Baytown, Texas, where he **restrained** the officers in the back of the van [...].* [ESC v1.0, 3_4, sentence 3]

In example 1, the event **quake** took place in 2004, a different (and distant) time period with respect to the actual **killing** in the sentence. Interestingly, we observe that such context dependent errors compose the majority of invalid False Positive up to 0.7. At 0.6 and 0.5, we have observed an increase of errors (or better disagreements) like example 2 where, rather than a misinterpretation of the context, it is the presence of the causal/explanatory relation itself that is in doubt or not valid. In this latter case, if we use a commonsense-based trigger question like "*why were the officers **restrained**?*", it is very unlikely to answer "*Because the escapee drove them. A more suitable answer would be "Because the escapee took the officers hostage.*

Finally, concerning the directionality of the relations, we measured the observed agreement of the pairs that both the experts and the crowd have annotated, using the same thresholds. Agreement ranges between 0.973 for threshold 1.0 and to 0.909 for threshold 0.5. At 0.7, we observed a score of 0.945. The trend is somehow parallel to the pairs detection, although these values signal an almost perfect "agreement" with the experts.

5 Conclusion and Future Work

This paper has reported on a crowdsourcing task for identifying causal relations between pairs of events. We adopted a loose definition of causality, that is best represented by contingent relations. By means of a pilot experiment we could identify the best amount of events to present to the workers in order to obtain as much as possible reliable annotations. We used the CrowdTruth metrics both to evaluate the quality of the annotated data and to weight the quality of the workers based on their overall agreement with the rest of the workers. This has allowed us to access diverse annotations, using "disagreement" as an extra source of information rather than to decide what is right or wrong. Finally, we have converted the crowd data in the same format of ESC v1.0 and generated flexible Gold Standard data, either by merging the crowd data per threshold to the experts or by using only the crowd data. We call this new resource ESC v1.2 and make it publicly available.

Natural languages have an extremely varied set of devices (i.e. granularity) to express relations among concepts, also for causal/contingent relations. Such relations are in most cases not explicitly marked in the sentence/text. As a further insight from the analysis of the crowd-expert pairs only (i.e. Table 4), we can observe that the causal relation task has different levels of complexity for the crowd. In particular, it appears that the identification of valid pairs of events is a harder task than the identification of the relation directionality.

The combined comparison with expert data has helped us to gain more insights on the differences in annotations between these two approaches. There is a general tendency for crowd workers to provide more valid annotations than experts, confirming previous studies (Caselli et al., 2016). At the same time, we can exploit the *SCausalRel* score to identify reliability thresholds of the annotated data. The differences in quality should not be considered as errors but rather as proxies for the complexity of the task and of the actual data in analysis. This calls for the development of new annotation procedures. We should reconsider using experts to generate annotations from scratch, and thus risking of making the generation of new datasets an infeasible task due to money, time, and effort. On the other hand, we should embrace the ability and diversity of the crowd to perform complex semantic tasks and promote a new allegiance between crowd and experts. As our results have shown, even at a threshold of 0.5, there is still a lot of valid information (in our case 49.65%) that should not be discarded and this is when we should employ experts. As lower thresholds signal also more complex data, experts should be employed in revising these data. This will result in richer, better, and possibly less biased datasets to be used as benchmarks for NLP systems.

As future work, we are planning to extend the ESC corpus with newly annotated data by applying the "crowd-experts-in-the-loop" approach in two directions. The first aims at collecting more data, and therefore, to allow the development or adaptation of NLP systems for storyline extraction. The second goal aims at extending the annotations in languages other than English, thus giving rise to a multilingual version of the ESC dataset.

References

Cem Akkaya, Alexander Conrad, Janyce Wiebe, and Rada Mihalcea. 2010. Amazon mechanical turk for subjectivity word sense disambiguation. In *Proceedings of the NAACL HLT 2010 workshop on creating speech and language data with Amazon's Mechanical Turk*, pages 195–203. Association for Computational Linguistics.

Lora Aroyo and Chris Welty. 2014. The three sides of crowdtruth. *Journal of Human Computation*, 1:31–34.

Lora Aroyo and Chris Welty. 2015. Truth is a lie: Crowd truth and the seven myths of human annotation. *AI Magazine*, 36(1):15–24.

Collin F Baker, Charles J Fillmore, and John B Lowe. 1998. The berkeley framenet project. In *Proceedings of the*

17th international conference on Computational linguistics-Volume 1, pages 86–90. Association for Computational Linguistics.

Mieke Bal. 1997. *Narratology: Introduction to the theory of narrative*. University of Toronto Press.

Brian Boyd. 2009. *On the origin of stories*. Harvard University Press.

Tommaso Caselli and Piek Vossen. 2016. The storyline annotation and representation scheme (star): A proposal. In *Proceedings of the 2nd Workshop on Computing News Storylines (CNS 2016)*, pages 67–72.

Tommaso Caselli and Piek Vossen. 2017. The event storyline corpus: A new benchmark for causal and temporal relation extraction. In *Proceedings of the Events and Stories in the News Workshop*, pages 77–86, Vancouver, Canada, August. Association for Computational Linguistics.

Tommaso Caselli, Rachele Sprugnoli, Oana Inel, et al. 2016. Temporal information annotation: Crowd vs. experts. In *LREC*.

Nathanael Chambers and Dan Jurafsky. 2008. Unsupervised learning of narrative event chains. *Proceedings of ACL-08: HLT*, pages 789–797.

Bernard Comrie. 1981. Causative constructions in language universals and linguistic typology.

Anca Dumitrache, Lora Aroyo, and Chris Welty. 2018. Capturing ambiguity in crowdsourcing frame disambiguation. *arXiv preprint arXiv:1805.00270*.

Jesse Dunietz, Lori Levin, and Jaime Carbonell. 2017. The because corpus 2.0: Annotating causality and overlapping relations. In *Proceedings of the 11th Linguistic Annotation Workshop*, pages 95–104.

Roxana Girju and Dan Moldovan. 2002. Mining answers for causation questions. In *Proc. The AAAI Spring Symposium on Mining Answers from Texts and Knowledge Bases*, pages 67–82.

Jonathan Gottschall. 2012. *The storytelling animal: How stories make us human*. Houghton Mifflin Harcourt.

Amit Goyal, Ellen Riloff, and Hal Daume III. 2010. Automatically producing plot unit representations for narrative text. In *Proceedings of the 2010 Conference on Empirical Methods in Natural Language Processing*, pages 77–86, Cambridge, MA, October. Association for Computational Linguistics.

JR Hobbs. 1985. Granularity (pp. 432–435). In *9th International Joint Conference on Artificial Intelligence, Los Angeles*, pages 18–23.

Dian Hu and David A Broniatowski. 2017. Measuring perceived causal relationships between narrative events with a crowdsourcing application on mturk. In *International Conference on Social Computing, Behavioral-Cultural Modeling and Prediction and Behavior Representation in Modeling and Simulation*, pages 349–355. Springer.

David Jurgens. 2013. Embracing ambiguity: A comparison of annotation methodologies for crowdsourcing word sense labels. In *Proceedings of the 2013 Conference of the North American Chapter of the Association for Computational Linguistics: Human Language Technologies*, pages 556–562.

Paul Kingsbury and Martha Palmer. 2002. From treebank to propbank. In *LREC*, pages 1989–1993. Citeseer.

Kenton Lee, Yoav Artzi, Yejin Choi, and Luke Zettlemoyer. 2015. Event detection and factuality assessment with non-expert supervision. In *Proceedings of the 2015 Conference on Empirical Methods in Natural Language Processing*, pages 1643–1648.

Wendy G Lehnert. 1981. Plot units and narrative summarization. *Cognitive Science*, 5(4):293–331.

Inderjeet Mani. 2012. Computational modeling of narrative. *Synthesis Lectures on Human Language Technologies*, 5(3):1–142.

George A Miller. 1995. Wordnet: a lexical database for english. *Communications of the ACM*, 38(11):39–41.

Paramita Mirza and Sara Tonelli. 2016. Catena: Causal and temporal relation extraction from natural language texts. In *Proceedings of COLING 2016, the 26th International Conference on Computational Linguistics: Technical Papers*, pages 64–75.

Nasrin Mostafazadeh, Nathanael Chambers, Xiaodong He, Devi Parikh, Dhruv Batra, Lucy Vanderwende, Pushmeet Kohli, and James Allen. 2016a. A corpus and evaluation framework for deeper understanding of commonsense stories.

Nasrin Mostafazadeh, Alyson Grealish, Nathanael Chambers, James Allen, and Lucy Vanderwende. 2016b. Caters: Causal and temporal relation scheme for semantic annotation of event structures. In *Proceedings of the Fourth Workshop on Events*, pages 51–61.

Rutu Mulkar-Mehta, Jerry Hobbs, and Eduard Hovy. 2011. Granularity in natural language discourse. In *Proceedings of the Ninth International Conference on Computational Semantics*, pages 360–364. Association for Computational Linguistics.

Rashmi Prasad, Eleni Miltsakaki, Nikhil Dinesh, Alan Lee, Aravind Joshi, Livio Robaldo, and Bonnie L Webber. 2007. The penn discourse treebank 2.0 annotation manual.

James Pustejovsky, José M Castano, Robert Ingria, Roser Sauri, Robert J Gaizauskas, Andrea Setzer, Graham Katz, and Dragomir R Radev. 2003. Timeml: Robust specification of event and temporal expressions in text. *New directions in question answering*, 3:28–34.

Karin Kipper Schuler. 2005. Verbnet: A broad-coverage, comprehensive verb lexicon.

Rion Snow, Brendan O'Connor, Daniel Jurafsky, and Andrew Y Ng. 2008. Cheap and fast—but is it good?: evaluating non-expert annotations for natural language tasks. In *Proceedings of the conference on empirical methods in natural language processing*, pages 254–263. Association for Computational Linguistics.

Maria Sukhareva, Judith Eckle-Kohler, Ivan Habernal, and Iryna Gurevych. 2016. Crowdsourcing a large dataset of domain-specific context-sensitive semantic verb relations. In *LREC*.

Leonard Talmy. 1976. Semantic causative types. *The grammar of causative constructions*, pages 43–116.

Piek Vossen, Tommaso Caselli, and Yiota Kontzopoulou. 2015. Storylines for structuring massive streams of news. In *Proceedings of the First Workshop on Computing News Storylines*, pages 40–49.

Phillip Wolff. 2007. Representing causation. *Journal of experimental psychology: General*, 136(1):82.

Can You Spot the Semantic Predicate in this Video?

Christopher Reale, Claire Bonial, Heesung Kwon and **Clare R. Voss**
U.S. Army Research Lab, Adelphi, Maryland 20783
`christopher.reale@gmail.com`
`{claire.n.bonial.civ, heesung.kwon.civ, clare.r.voss.civ}@mail.mil`

Abstract

We propose a method to improve human activity recognition in video by leveraging semantic information about the target activities from an expert-defined linguistic resource, VerbNet. Our hypothesis is that activities that share similar event semantics, as defined by the semantic predicates of VerbNet, will be more likely to share some visual components. We use a deep convolutional neural network approach as a baseline and incorporate linguistic information from VerbNet through multi-task learning. We present results of experiments showing the added information has negligible impact on recognition performance. We discuss how this may be because the lexical semantic information defined by VerbNet is generally not visually salient given the video processing approach used here, and how we may handle this in future approaches.

1   Introduction

Human activity recognition is a crucial component of comprehensive, multimodal event detection and identification as well as a prerequisite for more complex tasks, such as establishing timelines from video and video caption generation. In this work, we attempt to improve the performance of activity recognition in video by considering the event semantics associated with the activity types. Yatskar et al. (2016) have done this for images by leveraging a large dataset that is thoroughly labeled with the activity performed in each image, the actors involved, and the roles the actors play in the activity. While their method works well, it comes at the cost of obtaining and labeling the dataset. In this work, we eschew the use of an expensive labeled dataset and instead leverage the lexical semantic information found in VerbNet (VN) (Kipper et al., 2008) and only a small amount of manually annotated data.

Our hypothesis is that activities that share similar event semantics will be more likely to share some visual components. To begin to explore this hypothesis, we must first select the type and specificity of semantics that should be coupled with an activity. Here, we use VN to obtain semantic representations in the form of composed predicates, which apply to classes of verbs denoting more or less similar event types. The semantic representations therefore provide a level of generalization over somewhat distinct events. This extra information comes at the activity level rather than the sample level, and thus provides relatively weak supervision. Nonetheless, we feel our hypothesis intuitively holds promise and, if supported, would enable efficient improvement in activity recognition with less training data. Specifically, the ability to detect similar visual components across an event type could allow for generalizing from the recognition of one activity type (e.g., baseball pitch) to another that is semantically similar (e.g., throw discus).

2   Related Work

Human activity recognition is a heavily researched problem in computer vision. The goal is to determine the activity being performed in a video (e.g., walking, playing piano). This can be challenging due to the large range of appearances that videos of a given activity can take on. The problem is usually formulated as a classification task where each target video must be classified as one of a list of potential activities based on features extracted from its frames.

Proceedings of the Workshop on Events and Stories in the News, pages 55–60
Santa Fe, New Mexico, USA, August 20, 2018.

In addition to visible features extracted from videos, it is common to leverage external information from text, audio, or image data sets. Much work has been done investigating the relationship between text and imagery, though it has mainly focused on still images rather than videos. Recent work in this area has been spurred by the increasing availability of novel datasets, such as the visual question-answering research of Antol et al. (2015), which makes use of a dataset of open-ended natural language questions about images. On the video side, Motwani and Mooney (2012) use text mining and object recognition to help with activity recognition. Vondrick et al. (2016) leverage text captions to try to assign intent to human actions in video. To our knowledge, no work has been done to examine the relationship between event semantics in text-based lexical resources and videos.

3   Background to VerbNet

VerbNet,[1] based on the verb classification of Levin (1993), groups verbs into classes according to their compatibility with certain "diathesis alternations" or syntactic alternations (e.g., *She loaded the wagon with hay* vs. *She loaded hay into the wagon*). Although the groupings are primarily syntactic, the classes do share semantic features as well, since, as Levin posited, the syntactic behavior of a verb is largely determined by its meaning.[2] VN makes the shared semantics of a class explicit by including a semantic representation for each usage example demonstrating a characteristic diathesis alternation of a class. For example, in the Throw class, the following semantic representation would apply to this usage example:

        Ex.:"Maddox pitched the ball into the field."
        Roles: Agent Verb Theme Destination
        Semantic Predicates:
        CONTACT(during(E0), Agent, Theme)
        EXERT_FORCE(during(E0), Agent, Theme)
        not(CONTACT(during(E1), Agent, Theme))
        MOTION(during(E1), Theme)
        LOCATION(end(E1), Theme, Destination)
        not(LOCATION(start(E1), Theme, Destination))
        CAUSE(Agent, E1)

This representation is intended to break the event down into smaller semantic elements, given as the predicates (in caps). The predicates are organized with respect to the time of the event ('E'); thus they can apply during, at the start, or at the end of an event. The above representation can be paraphrased as expressing that Maddox (Agent) is in contact with and exerts force (E0) on the ball (Theme); he then releases (is not in contact with) the ball and the ball is in motion (E1); the ball's location at the end of the motion event is the field (Destination), where it was not located at the start of the event; Maddox causes this event as the Agent. Notice that although this representation captures many of the salient semantic components of a throwing event, it may not capture the salient visual aspects of a throwing events.

The numbered classes in VN are organized into a shallow taxonomy. Classes with shared semantic elements, and accordingly with shared subsets of the same semantic predicates, begin with the same class number. For example, Throw-17.1 and Pelt-17.2 form one "meta-class."

4   Data and Annotations

For video data, we chose to use the benchmark UCF101 dataset (Soomro et al., 2012) because of its wide variety of activities in comparison to other datasets. We then compared the coverage of the 101 activities in UCF to the types of events represented in VN. We selected four types of events of interest that had some overlap between UCF and VN: events involving motion with a vehicle (VN meta-class 51.4.X), throwing events (VN 17.X), hitting events (VN 18.X), and human group motion events (VN 51.3.2). Intuitively, we felt that each of these events had some clear visual properties associated with the semantics of the type (i.e. fairly clear, distinct image-schemas (Lakoff, 1990))

---

[1]VerbNet version 3.2 is used: https://verbs.colorado.edu/verb-index

[2]Levin's hypothesis continues to be debated, but efforts to crowdsource empirical evidence of the presence and saliency of the semantics in VN are promising (Hartshorne et al., 2014; Hartshorne et al., 2013).

One linguist and author of this paper, experienced with VN annotation, annotated each of the 101 UCF activity categories with an indication of whether or not the semantics of one of the four types was present in that activity. This was done by first completing a thorough review of the semantic representations found in the (meta-)classes for a given event type.[3] Then, a sample of 10-12 videos from each UCF activity category were observed to get a sense of the nature of actions included in an activity, and the variability of the clips included under a single category.[4] For each UCF category, one of the following indications was given: "Yes" the semantic elements of an event type are present in this activity, "No" the semantics are not present in the activity, or "maybe" the semantics are present in some videos of the activity but not in all. For example, video clips of the UCF activity Biking all include the semantics of motion with a vehicle, none include the semantics of throwing or hitting events, and some clips may include the semantics of group motion in video clips that show a group of cyclists. Additional examples are included in Table 1.[5]

UCF Activity	Vehicle Motion	Throwing	Hitting	Group Motion
ApplyEyeMakeup	no	no	no	no
Bowling	no	yes	maybe	no
Drumming	no	no	yes	no
Surfing	yes	no	no	no
MilitaryParade	no	no	no	yes
SkateBoarding	yes	no	no	no
Total "Yes"/"Maybe"/"No"	12/1/88	10/8/83	14/12/75	3/4/94

Table 1: Sample of annotation examples showing which UCF activities correspond to which event type. The "maybe" indicates some Bowling video clips that include the ball hitting pins. Annotations were completed for all 101 UCF activities, only six of these are shown here.

5 Experiment

We use the two-stream convolutional network approach of Simonyan and Zisserman (2014) as a baseline model.[6] In this model, two neural networks are trained to classify videos. The first is trained on the raw frames and the second on optical flow features extracted from the frames. Both networks are trained to classify the activities from small portions of the video (the visible network is trained on single frames, while the motion network is trained on five-frame segments). To test a video, 25 equally spaced frames are passed through the visual network and 25 equally spaced five-frame segments are passed through the motion network. The video is then classified as the activity with the highest average probability.

We alter the approach of Simonyan and Zisserman (2014) by injecting information from VN with multi-task learning (Caruana, 1993). Multi-task learning is the process of simultaneously training for several objectives. In our case, we train the networks to classify the VN class or meta-class the activities belong to in addition to the categories of the activities themselves.

5.1 Network and Training Details

We use the pre-trained (other than the final layer, which is randomly initialized) version of AlexNet (Krizhevsky et al., 2012) for the frame network. For the optical flow network, we use the structure of CNN-M 2048 of Chatfield et al. (2014) with random initialization. The networks are very similar in that both have five convolution layers followed by three fully connected layers. The main difference between the two (beyond initialization method) is that CNN-M 2048 is wider (more hidden nodes per layer).

---

[3]Note that we are focused on finding the presence or absence of particular semantic predicates (e.g., is there MOTION? is there CONTACT?), as opposed to certain participants or semantic roles. We are focusing on the latter in ongoing work.

[4]UCF includes 13320 videos, about 130 videos/activity.

[5]All annotations can be made available upon request.

[6]Many state-of-the-art activity recognition methods are offshoots of the two-stream approach of Simonyan and Zisserman (2014). For example, Feichtenhofer et al. (2016) experiment with early fusion of the two streams, and Wang et al. (2016) incorporate object detectors into the algorithm.

In order to incorporate information from VN, we create four extra tasks for the networks to solve. Each task is to determine whether or not a video belongs to one of the four chosen VN event types. We formulate this with a separate logistic regression loss for each event type. During training, for each event type, we treat activities labeled "yes" as positive samples, activities labeled "no" as negative samples, and ignore activities labeled "maybe."

All tasks share the first seven layers of the network (Conv1, Conv2, Conv3, Conv4, Conv5, FC6, and FC7). The last layer of the network is a fully connected (FC) layer that serves as a linear classifier for a given task, so it cannot be shared amongst them. Thus each objective has its own eighth (FC8) layer. See Figure 1 for a visual representation of the layout.

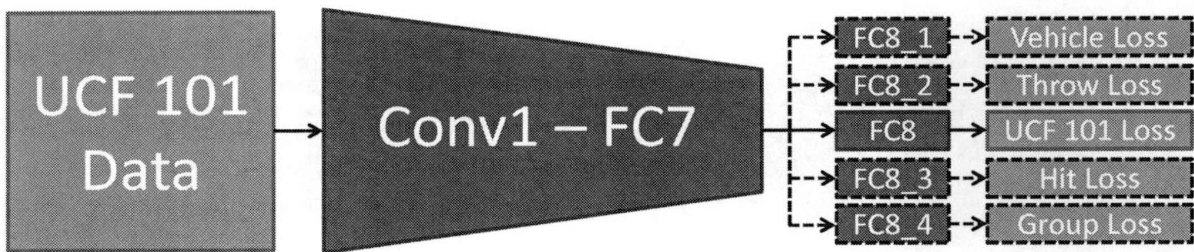

Figure 1: Multitask learning layout: the orange shapes represent loss functions, the blue shapes represent the network, and the green shape represents the input data. Sections outlined with dotted lines denote the additional multitask learning components.

We train the networks using the standard back-propagation algorithm and mini-batch stochastic gradient descent. We train the raw frame network for a total of 20,000 iterations. We start the learning rate at .01 and divide it by 10 after 14,000 iterations. Due to the random initialization, we must train the optical flow network for longer, and thus train it for 110,000 iterations. We start the learning rate at .01, and divide it by 10 after 50,000 and 100,000 iterations. When training both networks, we set the momentum to .9, the batch size to 256, and the weight decay to .0001. We use dropout in the first two fully connected layers (FC6 and FC7) of both networks with dropout rate of .5 for the frame network and .75 for the flow network.

5.2 Results

We ran two sets of experiments; we report results for the networks individually (as opposed to their fused performance) in order to examine which of the two networks (one trained on frames, the other on optical flow) is most affected by our method. For all experiments, we report the classification accuracy (i.e. percentage of videos matched to correct activity out of 101 choices) of the trained networks on the 3,783 test videos from split one of the of the UCF data set.

In the first set of experiments, we use all four VN classification objectives in addition to the primary UCF classification objective. We then train the networks with different values (0, 1, 2) for the relative weight given to the VN objectives. Table 2 compares the results when the VN objectives (All, All 2x Weight) are used and when they are not used (Baseline). When the weight is set to one, our method has a negligible effect on the performance compared to the baseline method (i.e. weight = 0). Increasing the weight to two causes the network performance to decrease.

In the second set of experiments, we train the networks with only one additional VN task at a time to see if some event types are more beneficial than others. All objectives were given the same weight in these experiments. In Table 2, we also compare the results of using one VN objective at a time (Vehicle Motion, Throwing, Hitting, Group Motion) to not using any of the VN objectives (Baseline). The extra VN tasks have little effect on the activity recognition performance compared to the baseline method.

We believe the main reason our method fails to provide significant improvement over the baseline is the lack of a relationship between the VN categories and visual appearance of the activities. For example, Bowling and BaseballPitch are both in the throwing category, but they are not necessarily visually similar—what portions of the actions are visually similar are likely not salient enough to be

VN Type	Frames	Optical Flow
All	67.14	77.07
All 2x Weight	61.33	76.47
Vehicle Motion	66.22	77.07
Throwing	66.32	77.27
Hitting	66.59	76.92
Group Motion	67.17	77.50
Baseline	67.08	77.13

Table 2: Performance comparison of our method to the baseline method (Baseline) which does not use any VN information. We evaluate our method using all four VN objectives at once (All), all at once but doubly weighted (All 2x Weight), and with one VN objective at a time (Vehicle Motion, Throwing, Hitting, Group Motion). All values denote the classification accuracy on the 3783 videos.

useful in the current video processing approach (see sample still images taken from the UCF101 dataset in Figure 2). Although our hypothesis was not supported using this approach, we have recourse to pursue this hypothesis in different ways. It may be that the semantic representation that we selected is adequate, but our video processing methodology is not, or that we need to select a different semantic representation more suited to the current video processing methodology.

Figure 2: Still images taken from video clips of Baseball Pitch and Bowling videos in UCF101 dataset (http://crcv.ucf.edu/data/UCF101.php). Although the event semantics of the two activities may share similarities, many visual aspects of the activities (e.g., the surroundings) are very different.

6   Conclusions & Future Work

Although a negative result, this is a notable finding: event-semantic similarity does not necessarily translate into visual similarity. In our next steps, we will ensure that the extra semantic information used to train our network is also visually salient. We plan to do this with a multi-task learning approach where, in addition to training the network to recognize the activities, we will also train it to recognize objects and entities that are frequently associated with the target activities. This will enable us to better recognize, for example, Bowling activities based on the recognition of a bowling ball and pins. We will leverage annotated text corpora to determine what objects most often fill a participant role slot, or semantic role, for the target activities. We will then use ImageNet (Deng et al., 2009) to train our systems to detect these objects.

References

Stanislaw Antol, Aishwarya Agrawal, Jiasen Lu, Margaret Mitchell, Dhruv Batra, C Lawrence Zitnick, and Devi Parikh. 2015. Vqa: Visual question answering. In *Proceedings of the IEEE International Conference on Computer Vision*, pages 2425–2433.

Richard Caruana. 1993. Multitask learning: A knowledge-based source of inductive bias. In *Proceedings of the Tenth International Conference on Machine Learning*, pages 41–48. Morgan Kaufmann.

K. Chatfield, K. Simonyan, A. Vedaldi, and A. Zisserman. 2014. Return of the devil in the details: Delving deep into convolutional nets. In *British Machine Vision Conference*.

Jia Deng, Wei Dong, Richard Socher, Li-Jia Li, Kai Li, and Li Fei-Fei. 2009. Imagenet: A large-scale hierarchical image database. In *Computer Vision and Pattern Recognition, 2009. CVPR 2009. IEEE Conference on*, pages 248–255. IEEE.

Christoph Feichtenhofer, Axel Pinz, and Andrew Zisserman. 2016. Convolutional two-stream network fusion for video action recognition. In *Proceedings of the IEEE Conference on Computer Vision and Pattern Recognition*, pages 1933–1941.

Joshua K Hartshorne, Claire Bonial, and Martha Palmer. 2013. The verbcorner project: Toward an empirically-based semantic decomposition of verbs. In *EMNLP*, pages 1438–1442.

Joshua K Hartshorne, Claire Bonial, and Martha Palmer. 2014. The verbcorner project: Findings from phase 1 of crowd-sourcing a semantic decomposition of verbs. In *ACL (2)*, pages 397–402.

Karin Kipper, Anna Korhonen, Neville Ryant, and Martha Palmer. 2008. A large-scale classification of english verbs. *Language Resources and Evaluation*, 42(1):21–40.

Alex Krizhevsky, Ilya Sutskever, and Geoffrey E Hinton. 2012. Imagenet classification with deep convolutional neural networks. In *Advances in neural information processing systems*, pages 1097–1105.

George Lakoff. 1990. The invariance hypothesis: is abstract reason based on image-schemas? *Cognitive Linguistics (includes Cognitive Linguistic Bibliography)*, 1(1):39–74.

Beth Levin. 1993. *English verb classes and alternations: A preliminary investigation*. University of Chicago press.

Tanvi S Motwani and Raymond J Mooney. 2012. Improving video activity recognition using object recognition and text mining. In *Proceedings of the 20th European Conference on Artificial Intelligence*, pages 600–605. IOS Press.

Karen Simonyan and Andrew Zisserman. 2014. Two-stream convolutional networks for action recognition in videos. In *Advances in neural information processing systems*, pages 568–576.

Khurram Soomro, Amir Roshan Zamir, and Mubarak Shah. 2012. Ucf101: A dataset of 101 human actions classes from videos in the wild. *arXiv preprint arXiv:1212.0402*.

C. Vondrick, D. Oktay, H. Pirsiavash, and A. Torralba. 2016. Predicting motivations of actions by leveraging text. In *2016 IEEE Conference on Computer Vision and Pattern Recognition (CVPR)*, pages 2997–3005, June.

Yifan Wang, Jie Song, Limin Wang, Luc Van Gool, and Otmar Hilliges. 2016. Two-stream sr-cnns for action recognition in videos. In *BMVC*, pages ***–***.

Mark Yatskar, Luke Zettlemoyer, and Ali Farhadi. 2016. Situation recognition: Visual semantic role labeling for image understanding. In *Proceedings of the IEEE Conference on Computer Vision and Pattern Recognition*, pages 5534–5542.

Fine-grained Structure-based News Genre Categorization

Zeyu Dai, Himanshu Taneja and Ruihong Huang
Department of Computer Science and Engineering
Texas A&M University
{zeyudai,himanshu27,huangrh}@tamu.edu

Abstract

Journalists usually organize and present the contents of a news article following a well-defined structure. In this work, we propose a new task to categorize news articles based on their content presentation structures, which is beneficial for various NLP applications. We first define a small set of news elements considering their functions (e.g., *introducing the main story or event, catching the reader's attention* and *providing details*) in a news story and their writing style (*narrative* or *expository*), and then formally define four commonly used news article structures based on their selections and organizations of news elements. We create an annotated dataset for structure-based news genre identification, and finally, we build a predictive model to assess the feasibility of this classification task using structure indicative features.

1 Introduction

There exist many guidelines for journalists in organizing and presenting contents in a news story. For example, when writing news briefs or breaking news, it is recommended to present the most newsworthy and key events first and then provide any additional details (e.g., sub-events of key events) (Po" ttker, 2003). While in other types of news, it is common to use a narrative hook (Myers and Wukasch, 2003) in the opening of a story that "hooks" the reader's attention so that the reader is willing to keep on reading the main story. Recognizing the overall structure of a news article can benefit many NLP tasks and applications, such as discourse parsing (Dijk, 1983), text segmentation, news summarization, information extraction and question answering system. Understanding the overall structure can also help reveal the events structure in the news. For example, the sequences of events in the news with *Narrative* structure usually follow the chronological order.

To categorize news articles based on their content organization and presentation differences, we first define a small set of news elements (section 3.1), and then formally define four commonly used news structures based on their different ways to select and organize news elements (section 3.2).

A news element is defined based on functions it plays in a news story as well as its writing style, and each news element is realized as a set of one or more consecutive paragraphs in a news article. The functions of a news element can be *introducing the main story and key events, catching the reader's attention* or *providing further details* etc.. We consider writing style in news stories as either *narrative* or *expository*. A narration section in a story usually describes surroundings, characters, and a sequence of events in a chronological order (Bal, 2009; Pentland, 1999; Smith, 2005), so that the reader can easily visualize the story with great details. An expository section is meant to provide information in a concise manner and usually answers the socalled *"5W1H"* questions: *what* are the events, *who* are involved, *where / when / why / how* did the events happen. Please see Table 1 for specific examples.

We then formally define four commonly used news structures (Wri, 2011; Jou, 2014; Po" ttker, 2003), *Inverted Pyramid, Kabob, Martini Glass* and *Narrative*, based on their selections and organizations of news elements. We then prepare annotation guidelines and create a dataset[1] containing around 900 news articles, where each article is annotated with its news structure and news elements. The annotated news

---

[1] The dataset will be made publicly available.

Proceedings of the Workshop on Events and Stories in the News, pages 61–67
Santa Fe, New Mexico, USA, August 20, 2018.

Functions: Introducing the Main Story and Key Event
(1) *Title: Harsh Storm Batters Island off the Coast of Russia*
Five days of blizzards and avalanches have paralyzed the Russian island of Sakhalin, cutting off air and sea links to the mainland, stranding dozens of motorists on highways, and burying a train, along with three railway workers, under snow drifts 10 feet deep.
Functions: Catching the Reader's Attention
(2) *Title: Twitter becomes a player in customer service world*

Have a problem with a business? Don't pick up the phone, or even log on to the company's Web site. Instead, Tweet it.
    Twitter, the 3-year-old social networking site, allows users to send 140-character text updates called "tweets" to groups of followers.
    "The modern-day consumer has gained considerable power and clout because of social media, and especially Twitter." says Larry Weintraub, CEO of Fanscape, a digital marketing agency. "Companies are on high alert, monitoring what people are saying about them in everyday conversations, or tweets."

Narrative writing style:
(3) The accident occurred March 28 as workers digging tunnels broke through a wall into an old shaft filled with water, flooding their V-shaped shaft. Five of the workers' nine platforms were submerged. The exit out of the pit was blocked. Of the 261 miners underground that day, 108 made it to safety. The rest were trapped and feared dead.
Expository writing style:
(4) Some 150 politicians, civil servants, tribal chiefs, police officers, Sunni clerics and members of Awakening Councils have been assassinated throughout Iraq since the election – bloodshed apparently aimed at heightening turmoil in the power vacuum created by more than three months without a national government.

Table 1: News Examples.

articles were sampled from four news domains, including *politics, crime, business* and *disaster* reports, for studying distributional differences of news structures across domains.

Finally, we design news structure indicative features and train a Support Vector Machine (SVM) (Cortes and Vapnik, 1995) classifier to label each news article with one of the proposed news structures. Experimental results show that reasonable performance can be achieved for automatic structure-based news genre classification by using our structure indicative features, even though results on minority classes remain low.

2 Related Work

The previous works on automated text categorization have considered various dimensions for categorization, such as *topic* (Kazawa et al., 2005; Zhou et al., 2009), *style* (Argamon-Engelson et al., 1998) and *author* (Stamatatos et al., 2000). Although news structures have been extensively studied in linguistics and journalism (Schokkenbroek, 1999; Van Dijk, 1985; Ytreberg, 2001), there are few studies trying to categorize a news article based on its content organization structure and there is no published dataset for developing such data-driven methods. To the best of our knowledge, we are the first to consider categorizing news articles according to news structures. Our main contributions include defining news elements and news structures, creating the first dataset for news structure identification as well as identifying news structure indicative features and conducting the first computational study for structure-based news genre categorization.

The well-studied text segmentation task (Ponte and Croft, 1997; Mulbregt et al., 1998; Dharanipragada et al., 1999) has focused on segmenting a document based on topics and identifying topic transition boundaries. Labov and Waletzky (2003) conducted an in-depth analysis of 14 narrative news stories and decomposed each story into six elements[2]. In contrast, we define a small set of news elements and determine the overall structure of each news based on the selection and organization of these elements.

3 Defining and Annotating News Structures

3.1 Five News Elements

We define each news element based on its functions in a news story and its writing style[3]. Based on their characteristics, we define five types of elements below:

Standard Lede: Located at the beginning of a news article; used to introduce the main story and key events to the reader in a very concise manner; written in the expository style; e.g., the first paragraph of example (1) in Table 1.

Image Lede: Located at the beginning of a news article; unlike Standard Lede, it does not directly discuss key events of the news, instead it catches the reader's attention by providing an anecdote related

---

[2]The six elements are abstract, orientation, complicating action, evaluation, resolution and coda.

[3]The two characteristics are often correlated.

to key events, quoting a catchy phrase or comment, or reporting an impressive fact or statistics (Jou, 2014); written in either narrative or expository style; e.g., the first paragraph of example (2) in Table 1.

Synopsis: Preceded by an Image Lede, the main purpose of Synopsis is to summarize the main story, inform the reader about key events and acts as a bridge between the Image Lede and the rest of the story; written in expository style; e.g., the second and third paragraphs of example (2) in Table 1.

Narration: Provides great details and often indicates the presence of a set of chronologically ordered events (Bal, 2009; Mani, 2012); written in narrative style; e.g., the example (3) in Table 1.

Body Section: Provides additional details and supplementary information about key events; written in expository style. Essentially, an element that does not belong to any of the above categories is annotated as a Body Section.

3.2 Four News Structures

News Structure	Inverted Pyramid	Martini Glass	Kabob	Narrative
First Element	Standard Lede	Standard Lede	Image Lede	Image Lede*
Second Element	Body Section	Body Section*	Synopsis	Narration
Third Element		Narration	Body Section	

Table 2: Element arrangement of each news article structure. * means this element is optional.

We distinguish four news structures based on their selections and organizations of news elements. Table 2 summarizes organization patterns of news elements for each news structure.

Inverted Pyramid (IP): *Inverted Pyramid* (Po¨ttker, 2003) as a news article structure has been widely used by newspapers since the beginning of the 20th century. In this news structure, contents are presented in the descending order of importance and relevance (Scanlan, 2003). It means that key events will be placed first, and additional details related to key events will be discussed later. Naturally, this structure can be represented as a *Standard Lede* followed by a *Body Section* as shown in Table 2.

Martini Glass (MG): Relied on a specific narrative chronology, *Martini Glass* (Wri, 2011; Jou, 2014) begins by presenting a summary of a story following the *Inverted Pyramid* structure, and then transitions into a detailed chronological elaboration of the story. This structure is better suited for stories that rely on a specific narrative chronology. Therefore, different from the *Inverted Pyramid* structure, a *Narration* element is included in the *Martini Glass* structure as well.

Kabob (Kab): In the *Kabob* (Wri, 2011; Jou, 2014) structure, a news story usually begins with an anecdote to catch the reader's attention, then introduces the main story and key events, and finally broadens into a general discussion with more details. Therefore, the *Kabob* structure starts with an *Image Lede*, and then uses a *Synopsis* as a transition followed by a *Body Section*.

Narrative (Nar): A narrative news story captivates the reader by presenting a chronologically ordered sequence of events with a greater amount of details than usual news. We label an article as *Narrative* if the majority paragraphs form a single *Narration* element with an optional preceding *Image Lede*.

Based on above definition, we can see that only the *Inverted Pyramid* and *Martini Glass* structures place key events of a news story at the beginning paragraphs; and only the *Martini Glass* and *Narrative* structures contain an Narration element written in narrative style. These commonalities and differences provide insights when designing features for categorizing news based on their structures.

3.3 Dataset Creation

To understand distributional differences of news structures across domains, we randomly sampled 250 documents for each of the four news domains, including *politics, crimes, business* and *disasters*, from the New York Times section of the Gigaword corpus (Robert Parker and Maeda, 2011) by matching news documents with pre-defined domain keywords[4]. Due to ambiguities of domain keywords, not every document is relevant to its deemed domain. Therefore, we manually checked the title of each document and cleaned the dataset by removing unrelated documents from each domain, in total, 147 documents

---

[4]We will list keywords in appendix.

were removed. In addition, we shifted 96 of the remaining news articles across domains. After cleaning, the dataset contains 853 news articles in total that span over four news domains.

We trained two annotators to annotate the dataset. For each document, annotators were asked to read the whole document and determine if it has one of the four news structures we defined, and then divide the document into segments corresponding to news elements. First, the two annotators annotated the same 170 documents for measuring annotation inter-agreements. Then, each annotator was asked to annotate half of the remaining documents. The two annotators achieved a Cohen's κ inter-agreement score of 67% in identifying the news structure type of each document and agreed on news element segmentations[5] for 61% of times.

3.4 Dataset Statistics

News Domains	Inverted Pyramid	Martini Glass	Kabob	Narrative	Other
Politics	154	17	53	10	6
Crime	113	12	61	32	8
Business	121	3	81	16	7
Disaster	94	5	42	18	0
Total	482	37	237	76	21

Table 3: News article structures distribution.

Table 3 shows the distribution of news structures in each domains and the overall distribution of news structures in our dataset. We can see that most of the annotated articles manifest one of the four news article structures we defined and the distribution of news structures is heavily imbalanced. As expected, the *Inverted Pyramid* is the dominant news article structure across the four domains, while there are the least number of news articles in the *Martini Glass* structure, mostly in the domains of *politics* and *crime*. Furthermore, depending on news domains, certain types of news article structures are more common. For example, there are more *crime* reports written in the *Narrative* structure compared with other news domains, while there are more *business* news articles in the structure of *Kabob*.

4 Automatic Structure-based News Genre Classification

We randomly selected 53 documents as the development set and trained a multi-class classifier using the remaining 800 documents with 10-fold cross-validation for predicting the news structure type of each news article. We use the implementation of the SVM model in LIBSVM (Chang and Lin, 2011) library with default settings and tuned hyper-parameters using the development set.

4.1 The Feature Set

N-gram Features: As basic features, we consider both unigrams and bigrams (Brown et al., 1992). Both were widely used in text classification tasks.

Writing Style Features: As we discussed in section 3.2, only the *Martini Glass* and *Narrative* structures include an Narration element, we therefore create two sets of features for recognizing narrative writing style. First, we create features for grammar production rules and we use the frequency of each syntactic production rule[6] (e.g., S $\rightarrow$ NP VP) extracted from constituency-based parse trees[7] as a feature. Second, we create a feature for each semantic category in LIWC (Linguistic Inquiry and Word Count) (Pennebaker et al., 2015) dictionary and the feature value is the occurrences of all words in that category. These LIWC features capture presences of certain types of words, such as words denoting

---

[5]We only count news elements that were annotated with exactly the same paragraph boundaries and the same news element type.

[6]Note that the bottom level syntactic production rules have the form of POS tag $\rightarrow$ WORD and contain a lexical word, which made these rules dependent on specific contexts. Therefore, we exclude these bottom level production rules to obtain more general features.

[7]We used Stanford CoreNLP (Manning et al., 2014) to generate constituency-based parse trees for each sentence.

relativity (e.g., motion, time, space), which were reported effective for detecting narrative stories (Yao and Huang, 2018).

Key Event Placement (KEP) Features: Note that only the *Inverted Pyramid* and *Martini Glass* structures start with a Standard Lede, which introduces key events directly and may repeat key events and associated event attributes (e.g., character, time and location) that were mentioned in the title as well. Therefore, we design a simple feature representing the number of words in overlap[8] between the first paragraph and news title.

4.2 Experimental Results

Feature Sets	IP	MG	Kab	Nar	Macro	Micro
Unigrams	71.6/85.1/77.8	0/0/0	51.3/43.4/47.1	53.2/35.2/42.4	44.0/40.9/41.8	65/65/65
Bigrams	71.6/87.1/78.6	0/0/0	53.6/44.3/48.5	52.5/29.6/37.8	44.4/40.3/41.2	66/66/66
Unigrams + Bigrams	72.5/87.5/79.3	0/0/0	56.5/45.2/50.3	58.0/40.8/47.9	46.7/43.4/44.4	67/67/67
+ Writing Style	73.4/85.8/79.1	37.5/9.1/14.6	56.3/48.4/52.1	62.0/43.7/**51.2**	57.3/46.7/49.3	68/68/68
+ KEP Features	74.7/88.4/81.0	0/0/0	56.4/48.0/51.8	55.8/40.8/47.2	46.7/44.3/45.0	69/69/69
+ Both	76.0/88.2/**81.7**	44.4/12.2/**19.1**	60.1/52.5/**56.0**	60.0/42.3/49.6	60.2/48.8/**51.6**	71/71/**71**

Table 4: 10-fold cross-validation classification results. Each cell shows Precision/Recall/F1 score.

Table 4 shows the experimental results using different groups of features. Using N-gram features only achieves good performance for recognizing the *Inverted Pyramid* structure. Added the writing style features on top of N-gram features significantly improves the classification performance on the *Martini Glass* and *Narrative* structures which contain a Narration element. Adding the KEP features further helps to identify three news article structures except the *Narrative* category. Note that the classification performance on the *Martini Glass* structure is poor, mainly because it is a minority class and not sufficiently represented in our dataset. We conclude that SVM model using both lexical features and our designed structure indicative features can achieve reasonable performance for predicting news article structure type.

5   Conclusion

We conducted the first study on fine-grained structure-based news genre categorization by defining a small set of general news elements and formally defining four commonly used news article structures. We created the first dataset of news articles annotated with both news structures and news elements. Finally, we conducted the initial experiments and showed the feasibility of automatic news genre categorization. Future work may include investigating the structure of event story within different news structure type.

Appendix

Here is the full list of domain keywords we used to sample news documents in Section 3.3:

Politics: [government, president, congress, white house, senate, Republican, GOP, Democratic, Tea Party, foreign minister, cabinet ministers];

Crime: [assasinate, arrest, bomb, murder, kidnap, robbery, manhunt, al qaeda, charged with assault, charged with battery];

Business: [merger, investor, stock, market, shareholders, hedge fund, banker, bankruptcy];

Disaster: [disaster management, weather warn, severe weather, x.x magnitude, wind speed, rescue team, volcano erupt, earthquake, oil spill].

References

Shlomo Argamon-Engelson, Moshe Koppel, and Galit Avneri. 1998. Style-based text categorization: What newspaper am i reading. In *Proc. of the AAAI Workshop on Text Categorization*, pages 1–4.

Mieke Bal. 2009. *Narratology: Introduction to the theory of narrative*. University of Toronto Press.

---

[8] Stop words were removed.

Peter F Brown, Peter V Desouza, Robert L Mercer, Vincent J Della Pietra, and Jenifer C Lai. 1992. Class-based n-gram models of natural language. *Computational linguistics*, 18(4):467–479.

Chih-Chung Chang and Chih-Jen Lin. 2011. LIBSVM: A library for support vector machines. *ACM Transactions on Intelligent Systems and Technology*, 2:27:1–27:27. Software available at http://www.csie.ntu.edu.tw/~cjlin/libsvm.

Corinna Cortes and Vladimir Vapnik. 1995. Support-vector networks. *Machine learning*, 20(3):273–297.

S Dharanipragada, M Franz, Jeffrey S McCarley, S Roukos, and Todd Ward. 1999. Story segmentation and topic detection in the broadcast news domain. In *Proceedings of the DARPA Broadcast News Workshop*, pages 65–68. Herndon: National Institute of Standar and Technology.

Teun A Dijk. 1983. Discourse analysis: Its development and application to the structure of news. *Journal of communication*, 33(2):20–43.

2014. Journalism story structure. http://journalism-education.cubreporters.org/2010/08/journalism-story-structure.html.

Hideto Kazawa, Tomonori Izumitani, Hirotoshi Taira, and Eisaku Maeda. 2005. Maximal margin labeling for multi-topic text categorization. In *Advances in neural information processing systems*, pages 649–656.

William Labov and Joshua Waletzky. 2003. *Narrative analysis: Oral versions of personal experience*. University of Washington Press.

Inderjeet Mani. 2012. Computational modeling of narrative. *Synthesis Lectures on Human Language Technologies*, 5(3):1–142.

Christopher Manning, Mihai Surdeanu, John Bauer, Jenny Finkel, Steven Bethard, and David McClosky. 2014. The stanford corenlp natural language processing toolkit. In *Proceedings of 52nd annual meeting of the association for computational linguistics: system demonstrations*, pages 55–60.

Paul van Mulbregt, Ira Carp, Lawrence Gillick, Steve Lowe, and Jon Yamron. 1998. Text segmentation and topic tracking on broadcast news via a hidden markov model approach. In *Fifth International Conference on Spoken Language Processing*.

Jack Myers and Don C Wukasch. 2003. *Dictionary of poetic terms*. University of North Texas Press.

James W Pennebaker, Ryan L Boyd, Kayla Jordan, and Kate Blackburn. 2015. The development and psychometric properties of liwc2015. Technical report.

Brian T Pentland. 1999. Building process theory with narrative: From description to explanation. *Academy of management Review*, 24(4):711–724.

Horst Po¨ttker. 2003. News and its communicative quality: The inverted pyramidwhen and why did it appear? *Journalism Studies*, 4(4):501–511.

Jay M Ponte and W Bruce Croft. 1997. Text segmentation by topic. In *International Conference on Theory and Practice of Digital Libraries*, pages 113–125. Springer.

Junbo Kong Ke Chen Robert Parker, David Graff and Kazuaki Maeda. 2011. English gigaword fifth edition.

Chip Scanlan. 2003. Writing from the top down: Pros and cons of the inverted pyramid. https://www.poynter.org/news/writing-top-down-pros-and-cons-inverted-pyramid.

Christina Schokkenbroek. 1999. News stories: structure, time and evaluation. *Time & Society*, 8(1):59–98.

Carlota S Smith. 2005. Aspectual entities and tense in discourse. In *Aspectual inquiries*, pages 223–237. Springer.

Efstathios Stamatatos, Nikos Fakotakis, and George Kokkinakis. 2000. Automatic text categorization in terms of genre and author. *Computational linguistics*, 26(4):471–495.

Teun A Van Dijk. 1985. Structures of news in the press. *Discourse and communication: New approaches to the analysis of mass media discourse and communication*, 10:69.

2011. Writing the article: Leads, quotes, and organization. https://springfieldnews.wikispaces.com/Writing+the+Article+--+Leads,+Quotes,+and+Organization.

Wenlin Yao and Ruihong Huang. 2018. Temporal event knowledge acquisition via identifying narratives. In *Proceedings of the 56th Annual Meeting of the Association for Computational Linguistics (Volume 1: Long Papers)*, volume 1.

Espen Ytreberg. 2001. Moving out of the inverted pyramid: narratives and descriptions in television news. *Journalism Studies*, 2(3):357–371.

Shibin Zhou, Kan Li, and Yushu Liu. 2009. Text categorization based on topic model. *International Journal of Computational Intelligence Systems*, 2(4):398–409.

On Training Classifiers for Linking Event Templates

Jakub Piskorski[1], Fredi Šarić[2], Vanni Zavarella[1], Martin Atkinson[1]
[1]Text and Data Mining Unit, Joint Research Centre of the European, Ispra, Italy
`{firstname.lastname}@ec.europa.eu`
[2]Text Analysis and Knowledge Engineering Lab, University of Zagreb, Croatia
`fredi.saric@fer.hr`

Abstract

The paper reports on exploring various machine learning techniques and a range of textual and meta-data features to train classifiers for linking related event templates automatically extracted from online news. With the best model using textual features only we achieved 94.7% (92.9%) F1 score on GOLD (SILVER) dataset. These figures were further improved to 98.6% (GOLD) and 97% (SILVER) F1 score by adding meta-data features, mainly thanks to the strong discriminatory power of automatically extracted geographical information related to events.

1 Introduction

With the rapid proliferation of large digital archives of textual information on what happens in the world, a need has raised recently to apply effective techniques that go beyond the classification and retrieval of text documents in response to profiled queries. Systems already exists that automatically distill structured information on events from free texts, e.g. with the goal of monitoring disease outbreaks (Yangarber et al., 2008), crisis situations (King and Lowe, 2003) and other security-related events from online news.

Classical event extraction engines typically extract knowledge by locally matching predefined event templates in text documents, by filling template slots with detected entities. However, when not coupled with modules for event co-reference detection, these systems tend to suffer of the event duplication problem, consisting of extracting several mentions referring to the same occurring event. That makes their output misleading for both real-time situation monitoring and long-term data aggregation and analysis.

While event co-reference is a semantically well-defined relationship (Mitamura et al., 2015), capturing some additional kinds of relationships, although more fuzzy, that link together events, may be crucial in order to reduce the information overload of the user of an event extraction engine.

Imagine a scenario where, given a large set of news reports about a major Terrorist Attack event, an event extraction engine returns a number of event templates like the ones shown in Figure 1. As it can be noticed from Title and Text of the source articles, while templates a. and b. describe the same main fact (the attack itself), c. provides updates on some police operations following it, d. tells about some public reactions to the event, while e. is about an official claiming of the attack by one terrorist organization. Recognizing a. and b. as duplicate reporting of the same event would help mitigating the information redundancy in the system. At the same time, while c., d. and e. should be regarded as semantically distinct events from a., extracting them as independent templates would result in a loss of information preventing a data user to obtain a complete picture of the ongoing situation. On the contrary, we envision an user-centered process, where an analyst is fed with a target event template and is allowed to explore on demand additional event templates, by calling an on-the-fly computation of related events in order to update the information from the original record.

In this context, we explore the possibility to merge a number of distinct event-event relationships (Caselli and Vossen, 2017) into a more general, user-centered definition of event linking, and experiment on training statistical classifiers for automatically detecting those links based on textual and non-textual content of event templates.

Proceedings of the Workshop on Events and Stories in the News, pages 68–78
Santa Fe, New Mexico, USA, August 20, 2018.

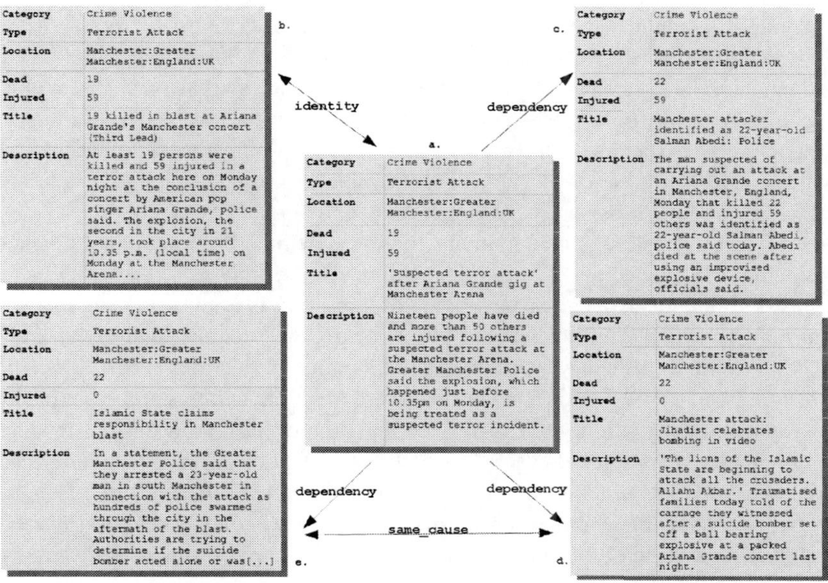

Figure 1: Event templates extracted from news reports following the 2017 Manchester terrorist attack, and the different relations linking them to the initial event report in a.

The motivation behind our work is four fold. Firstly, we are interested in elaboration of techniques for linking event information in existing event datasets, such as the one presented in (Atkinson et al., 2017), in order to improve their usability by the analysts. Therefore we have exploited this corpus to carry out the presented work. Secondly, as the event extraction engine underlying the (Atkinson et al., 2017) corpus is multilingual, we focus on exploring linguistically-lightweight event similarity metrics. Thirdly, we are interested in exploring how inclusion of automatically extracted event meta data (e.g., location) impacts the performance of the trained event linking models. Finally, due to scarcity of publicly available resources for carrying out research on event linking our intention was to contribute to the provision of such a resource, focusing particularly on creating a dataset that resembles a real-world scenario of event data for analysts, who are primarily interested in having access to all relevant event information rather than being provided with fine-grained labeling of event relations (e.g., temporal and causal).

Event linking has been modeled as the task of matching monolingual clusters of news articles, describing the same event, across languages. For example (Rupnik et al., 2017) use a number of techniques, including Canonical Correlation Analysis, exploiting comparable corpora such as Wikipedia. Work similar to ours was performed in the context of the event co-reference resolution task, that consists of clustering of event mentions that refer to the same event (Bejan et al., 2010). We diverge from both task formulations in that our underlying representation of events is richer than local event mentions, including meta-data and text slots from clusters of articles. (Weiwei Guo et al., 2013) proposes a task of linking tweets with news articles to enable other NLP tools to better understand Twitter feeds. Related work to event linking was also reported in (Nothman et al., 2012; Krause et al., 2016; Vossen et al., 2016).

The paper is structured as follows. Section 2 gives an overview of the event linking task. The event similarity metrics explored are introduced in Section 3. Subsequently, the experiments set-up and evaluation results are presented in Section 4. Finally, we end up with conclusions in Section 5.

2   Task description

The Event Linking task is defined as follows: given an event e and a set of events $E = \{e_1, ..., e_n\}$ compute $E^* = \{E^R, E^U\}$ a partition of E into two disjoint subsets of **related** (E^R) and **unrelated** (E^U) events to e. Each event e is associated with an event template $Temp(e)$ consisting of attribute-value pairs describing e, some of which are mandatory, e.g., TYPE, CATEGORY and LOCATION of the event, and optional event-specific ones, e.g., PERPETRATOR, WEAPONS_USED. An event template contains three string-valued mandatory slots, namely, TITLE, DESCRIPTION and SNIPPET which contain in the resp. order: the title and the first two sentences from the body of a news article on the event[1], and some text snippet that triggered the extraction of the event. Please refer to (Atkinson et al., 2017) for more details.

Figure 1 shows a simplified version of a target event template (a.), and a number of additional templates (b. through e.), all belonging to the subset of events related to a.

The semantics of the **related** relationship in our context is defined in a rather broad manner. An event $e' \in E$ is considered to be related to e if the corresponding event templates $Temp(e)$ and $Temp(e')$ refer to: (a) the same event (identity), (b) reporting about different aspects of the same ongoing situation/focal event (co-occurrence), (c) two events, where one event occurrence is temporally following and is induced by that of the other event (dependency) with an explicit mention of the prior event, e.g., a trial following a man-made disaster, and (d) two distinct events that were triggered by the same event (same cause).

Due to the application scenario sketched in Section 1, the event linking task is modeled here as a classification task applied over a set of events E which does not coincide with the whole search space of events gathered over time, but is rather a subset thereof retrieved as some function of the target event e (e.g., events within the same time window as e). This differentiates our approach from clustering methods that attempt to build a partition of the entire event search space based on some relatedness criteria.

3 Event Similarity Metrics

3.1 Text-based Metrics

For determining semantic similarity of text-based event slots we exploit a wide range of similarity measures, including, i.a., string similarity metrics, measures that exploit knowledge bases (e.g., WORDNET, BABELNET), and corpus-based similarity metrics. We did not explore measures not easily portable across languages, e.g., ones relying on syntactic parsing (Šarić et al., 2012). The remainder of this section introduces each of the measures used. Let T_1 and T_2 denote two texts being compared.

Levenshtein Distance (LT) is well-known edit distance metric given by the minimum number of character-level operations needed to transform one text into another (Levenshtein, 1965).

Longest Common Substrings (LCS) is a similarity distance metric, which recursively finds and removes the longest common sub-string in the two texts compared (Navarro, 2001). Let $lcs(T_1, T_2)$ denote the first longest common sub-string in T_1 and T_2 and let T_{i-p} denote a text obtained by removing from T_i the first occurrence of p in T_i. The LCS metric is then calculated as follows.

$$LCS(T_1, T_2) = \begin{cases} 0, & \text{if } |lcs(T_1, T_2)| < 3 \\ \frac{|lcs(T_1,T_2)|}{max(|T_1|,|T_2|)} + LCS(T_{1-lcs(T_1,T_2)}, T_{2-lcs(T_1,T_2)}), & \text{otherwise} \end{cases} \tag{1}$$

Word Ngram Overlap (WNO) is a fraction of common word ngrams in both texts and is defined as:

$$WordNgramOverlap(T_1, T_2) = \frac{2 \cdot |Ngrams(T_1) \cap Ngrams(T_2)|}{|Ngrams(T_1)| + |Ngrams(T_2)|} \tag{2}$$

where $Ngrams(T_i)$ denotes the set of consecutive ngrams in T_i. In particular, we computed ngram overlap for unigrams **WNO-1**, bigrams **WNO-2** and trigrams **WNO-3**.

Weighted Word Overlap (WWO) measures the overlap of words between the two texts, where words bearing more content are assigned higher weight (Šarić et al., 2012) using the following formula.

$$InfoContent(w) = \ln \frac{\sum_{x \in C} frequency(x)}{frequency(w)} \tag{3}$$

where C and $frequency(x)$ denote the set of words in the corpus and the frequency of x in C resp. The word frequencies were computed using the entire event corpus introduced in (Atkinson et al., 2017). We then define *Weighted Word Coverage (WWC)* of T_2 in T_1 as follows.

---

[1]The centroid article of the cluster of articles from which the event template was extracted

$$WWC(T_1, T_2) = \frac{\sum_{w \in Words(T_1) \cap Words(T_2)} InfoContent(w)}{\sum_{x \in Words(T_2)} InfoContent(x)} \tag{4}$$

where $Words(T_i)$ denotes the set of words occurring in T_i. The $WeightedWordOverlap(T_1, T_2)$ is then computed as the harmonic mean of $WWC(T_1, T_2)$ and $WWC(T_2, T_1)$.

Named-Entity Overlap (NEO) is a metric that computes similarity of the named entities found in both texts. Let us first define *Named-Entity Coverage (NEC)* of T_1 in T_2 as follows.

$$NEC(T_1, T_2) = \frac{1}{|Names(T_1)|} \cdot \sum_{n \in Names(T_1)} max_{m \in Names(T_2)} sim(n, m) \tag{5}$$

where $Names(T_i)$ denotes the set of named entities found in T_i and $sim(n, m)$ denotes a similarity score of n and m. The $NamedEntityOverlap(T_1, T_2)$ is then defined as harmonic mean of $NEC(T_1, T_2)$ and $NEC(T_2, T_1)$. In order to compute $sim(n, m)$ we used a weighted version of the LCS metric called *Weighted Longest Common Substrings*[2] introduced in (Piskorski et al., 2009).

For recognising names a combination of 3 lexico-semantic resources have been used in the respective order on the unconsumed part of the text: (a) JRC Variant Names database (ca. 4 mln entries) (Ehrmann et al., 2017), (b) a collection of multi-word named entities from BABELNET (Navigli et al., 2012) (ca. 6.8 mln entries) that have been semi-automatically derived using the method described in (Chesney et al., 2017), and (c) toponyms (only populated places) from the GeoNames[3] gazetteer (ca. 1.4 mln entries). Additionally, heuristics are used to join adjacent NEs. The aforementioned lexical resources cover a wide range of languages and the metric as such can be directly used on texts in other non-inflected languages.

Hypernym Overlap (HO) is an overlap of the set of hypernyms associated with named entities and concepts found in the texts being compared. Let $T = t_1 \ldots t_n$ and $S = s_1 \ldots s_n$ denote two texts, where $t_i(s_i)$ denote tokens. Further, let T^* and S^* denote the set of potentially overlapping text fragments (i.e., sequences of tokens) in T and S resp. which can be associated either with a named entity or a concept encoded in a knowledge base. The aforementioned text fragments are computed by identifying at each position in a text the longest sequence of tokens that can be associated with a name or concept. In particular, for computing the sets T^* and S^* we exploit version 3.6 of BABELNET (Navigli et al., 2012)[4]. The hypernym coverage of T in S is then defined as follows:

$$HypCoverage(T, S) = \frac{1}{|T^*|} \cdot \sum_{t \in T^*} \max_{s \in S^*} hypSim(t, s) \tag{6}$$

where $hypSim(t, s)$ denotes the hypernym similarity between t and s and is computed as follows:

$$hypSim(t, s) = \begin{cases} 1, & t = s \\ x, & \alpha + \beta \cdot \frac{|hyp(t) \cap hyp(s)|}{|hyp(t) \cup hyp(s)|} \\ 0, & hyp(t) \cap hyp(s) = \emptyset \end{cases} \tag{7}$$

where $hyp(s)$ denotes the hypernyms for s returned by BabelNet and α and β has been set to 0.2 and 0.5 resp. based on empirical observations. Finally, we define hypernym overlap between T and S as weighted harmonic mean of $HypCoverage(S, T)$ and $HypCoverage(T, S)$.

WordNet Similarity Word Overlap (WSWO) is a metric that exploits semantic similarity of word pairs computed using WORDNET[5]. To be more precise, we compute for each word in a one text a word in the second one with maximum semantic similarity and then normalise the sum of such similarity scores. We first define *WordNet Coverage (WNC)* of T_1 in T_2 as follows.

$$WNC(T_1, T_2) = \frac{1}{|Words(T_1)|} \cdot \sum_{w_1 \in Words(T_1)} \max_{w_2 \in Words(T_2)} sim(w_1, w_2) \tag{8}$$

---

[2]Common substrings closer to the beginning of the text are scored higher.
[3]http://www.geonames.org/
[4]For computing hypernyms we used BabelNet API method which returns all hypernyms for a given synset (depth one).
[5]We deployed the WS4j library for this purpose: https://github.com/Sciss/ws4j

where $sim(w_1, w_2)$ denotes WordNet-based semantic similarity measure between w_1 and w_2. In particular, we explored the following measures: **Path**[6], **WP** (Wu and Palmer, 1994), **Lesk** (Banerjee and Pedersen, 2002) and **HirstStOnge, LeacockChodorow, Resnik, JiangConrath** and **Lin** (Budanitsky et al., 2001). Finally, $WSWO(T_1, T_2)$ is defined as harmonic mean of $WNC(T_1, T_2)$ and $WNC(T_2, T_1)$.

Numerical Overlap is an overlap of the set of numerical expressions found in the texts being compared. While reported features for computing "similarity" of sets of numerical expressions do not differentiate between the specific types of such expressions (Socher et al., 2011) we do exploit numerical expression type information. To be more precise, all recognized numerical expressions are classified into one of the following categories: currency (e.g. *200mln$*), percentage, measurement (*one million kilograms*), age (e.g. *20-year-old*), number (e.g. *20 thousand*), whereas numbers being part of temporal references (e.g. *1 May 2017*) are discarded. Let $Num(T_i)$ denote the set of numerical expressions found in T_i. We then define **Absolute Numerical Overlap (ANO)** as follows.

$$AbsoluteNumericalOverlap(T_1, T_2) = \frac{2 \cdot |Num(T_1) \cap Num(T_2)|}{|Num(T_1)| + |Num(T_2)|} \tag{9}$$

We then define closeness of numerical expressions in T_i with numerical expressions in T_2 as follows.

$$NumericalCloseness(T_1, T_2) = \frac{1}{|Num(T_1)|} \cdot \sum_{t \in T_1} \max_{s \in T_2} closeness(t, s) \tag{10}$$

where $closeness(t, s)$ is defined as follows.

$$closeness(t, s) = \begin{cases} 1 - \log_2(1 + \frac{|t-s|}{\max(t,s)}), & type(t) = type(s) \\ 0, & type(t) \neq type(s) \end{cases} \tag{11}$$

Finally, we define **Relative Numerical Overlap (RNO)** between T_1 and T_2 as a weighted harmonic mean of $NumericalCloseness(T_1, T_2)$ and $NumericalCloseness(T_2, T_1)$.

Cosine of Text Vectors (CTV) is computed as $Cosine(Doc2Vec(T_1), Doc2Vec(T_2)$, where $Doc2Vec(T_i) = \frac{1}{|T_i|} \sum_{w \in T_i} embedding(w)$ (Le and Mikolov, 2014) is computed using Glove (Pennington et al., 2011) word embeddings.

3.1.1 Text Preprocessing

In the case of most of the metrics we deploy pre-processing of the text, which mainly boils down to: (a) lowercasing it, (b) normalising whitespaces, (c) removing constructs such as urls, etc. As regards WNO, $WSWO$ and WWO some initial/final token characters are stripped (e.g., brackets), while for computing $WSWO$, WWO and CVT one removes stop words using a list of ca. 250 English word forms. In the case of NEO and HO the texts are not downcased since this might have had deteriorated NE recognition performance which relies on orthographic features. For computing ANO and RNO no pre-processing is carried since non-alphanumeric characters often constitute part of numerical expressions.

3.2 Meta-data based Metrics

As regards meta-data information we define four metrics that exploit event location, category and type information. Since the reported quality of extraction of event-type specific slots (e.g. number of injured, perpetrators, etc.) is not very high we decided not to exploit such information in the experiments.

Location Administrative Similarity (LSA) computes the administrative distance between locations. It is a modification of WUP metric presented in (Wu and Palmer, 1994) and it aims to reflect how close two locations are with respect to an administrative hierarchy of geographical references. Let T_{GEO} denote the 4-level (Country, Region, Province and Populated Place) administrative hierarchy in the GeoNames gazetteer[7] and let $lcs(x, y)$ denote the lowest common subsumer for nodes x and y in T_{GEO} and $Loc(e)$ denote the node in T_{GEO} that corresponds to the location of the event e. LSA is then defined as follows:

---

[6]Counting the length of the path in 'is-a' Verb and Noun hierarchy
[7]http://www.geonames.org

TITLE: *Militants attack police party in Srinagar*
DESCRIPTION: *Two cops were injured tonight when militants attacked a police party in the Hyderpora area of the city here, police said. Unidentified militants fired upon a night police party near the branch in Hyderpora tonight, resulting in injuries to two policemen, a police official said.*

TITLE: *Civilian gunned down by militants in J-Ks Pulwama, 3rd death this week*
DESCRIPTION: *This was the third civilian killed in firing incidents this week. Earlier, one civilian was killed in Srinagars Rangreth area as security personnel allegedly opened fire to disperse stone-pelters, while another died during an encounter in Arwani village in Bijbehara area.*

Figure 2: An example of two events perpetrated by the same group as part of the same armed conflict.

$$LSA(e_1, e_2) = \frac{2 \cdot \omega(lcs(Loc(e_1), Loc(e_2)))}{\omega(Loc(e_1)) + \omega(Loc(e_1))} \tag{12}$$

where $\omega(v) = \sum_{i=0}^{depth(v)} \delta/2^i$ is a weighted depth of a node v in T_{GEO}, with δ empirically set to 10. The intuition behind LSA is to apply a higher weight to path segments closer to the root of T_{GEO}, e.g., distance paths at the Country level are penalized more than paths at the level of Province.

Location Geographical Similarity (LSG) computes geographical distance between two event locations:

$$LSG(e_1, e_2) = (\ln(dist(coord(e_1), coord(e_2)) + e))^{-1} \tag{13}$$

where $coord(e)$ denotes the coordinates of the location of the event e as found in the GEONAMES gazetteer, and $dist(p_1, p_2)$ denotes the physical distance in km. between the points p_1 and p_2.

Event Category Similarity (ECS) and **Event Type Similarity (ETS)** are two metrics that exploit the event category and type information. Let $cat(e)$ and $type(e)$ denote event category and type resp. The metrics are then defined as follows.

$$EventCategorySimilarity(e_1, e_2) = Prob(RELATED(e_1, e_2)|(cat(e_1), cat(e_2)) \tag{14}$$
$$EventTypeSimilarity(e_1, e_2) = Prob(RELATED(e_1, e_2)|(type(e_1), type(e_2)) \tag{15}$$

The respective probabilities for category and type pairs have been computed using the GOLD dataset (see Section 4.1). In case certain combination of types (categories) was not observed the respective probability was set to zero, whereas in case the type/category equality the resp. probability was set to 1.

4 Experiments

4.1 Dataset

We built 2 corpora consisting of event template pairs taken from the event dataset described in (Atkinson et al., 2017) and labeled as either related or unrelated. First, we attempted to create balanced groups of event templates, where initial groups were built by extracting events (not less than 5) around keys consisting of a category, location (country) and a timeslot (e.g. time window of +- 2 days) in 2017. Each of such initial groups G was subsequently amended with a set of max. $|G|/6$ most 'similar' events from the same time window and another set of max. $|G|/6$ most 'similar' events from 2017, but outside of the original time window. The events were selected through computing cosine similarity with the centroid template in G[8]. Finally, G was amended by adding $|G|/3$ of randomly selected events (disjoint from the previous groups) from the same time window, regardless of location, category and similarity.

For each resulting group, all event pairs were computed, which were then labeled by 4 annotators, who were asked to consider only textual and meta-data information in the templates. The average pairwise κ score for inter-annotator agreement on a sample of around 13.4K event pairs was over 0.85. Questionable cases were typically due to event granularity issues. For example, the two events in Figure 2 were arguably perpetrated by the same armed group as part of a same armed conflict in the same day and larger area. Whether the two killing incidents should be considered as different consequences of the same larger armed conflict event and thus be considered as related, or should they be considered as distinct events sharing a large number of slot values is an open question.

---

[8]Vector representations of event templates and thus centroid templates of groups are derived by computing Doc2Vec on joined DESCRIPTION, TITLE and SNIPPET textual slot and converting each word with GloVe word embeddings (Pennington et al., 2011)

Corpus	#RELATED	#UNRELATED	#CRI-VIO	#CIV-POL	#MM-DIS	#NAT-DIS	#MIL
GOLD	10705	6074	76.0%	3.65%	12.71%	4.0%	3.65%
SILVER	10606	11060	67.47%	7.0%	16.45%	4.15%	4.89%

Table 1: GOLD/SILVER dataset statistics. The first 2 columns provide number of related (unrelated) event pairs, the others provide % of events falling into: crisis-violence (CRI-VIO), civic-political action (CIV-POL), man-made disasters (MM-DIS), natural disasters (NAT-DIS) and military actions (MIL).

We used pairs with at least 2 non-conflicting judgments to build a GOLD dataset, whereas SILVER dataset was created on top of it through adding event pairs annotated only by one annotator. Detailed statistics are provided in Table 1.

4.2 Discriminative power of the Event Similarity Metrics

In order to have a preliminary insight into the discriminative power of the various event similarity metrics we exploit an objective measure $absDistance$. Let for some event similarity metric histogram h, $\{u_h\}$ and $\{r_h\}$ denote the sequences of heights of the bars for 'unrelated' and 'related' event pairs resp. for all considered bins $i \in I$. $absDistance$ is then defined as follows.

$$absDistance(h) = \sum_{i \in I} |u_i^h - r_i^h|/200 \qquad (16)$$

This metric computes the fraction of the area under the histogram curves being compared that corresponds to the symmetric difference between them, where the area under each histogram has 100 units. The higher values of $absDistance$ indicate better discriminative power of a metric being considered.

We have considered five different modes as regards computation of the features corresponding to the text-based event similarity metrics, namely: (a) only event description with the snippet is used (D), (b) only event title is used (T), (c) in addition to (a) the title is exploited as well (D+T), (d) similarity score for the title and description/snippet is computed separately and an average thereof is returned (AVG(D,T)), and (e) similarity score for the title and description/snippet is computed separately and the maximum of the two is returned (MAX(D,T)).

Figure 3 provides a comparison of the discriminative power computed using $absDistance$ on GOLD dataset for all event similarity metrics and four aforementioned modes in which text-based metrics are calculated. One can observe high potential of some of the meta-data metrics, namely LSG (more than 90% of the AUC) and ETS (more than 30% of the AUC), whereas NEO and WWO (both of which can be computed efficiently) lead the ranking of text-based metrics followed by metrics exploiting WORD-NET, BABELNET which also have relatively high discriminatory power (in the range of 45% - 80% of the AUC). In particular, HO discriminative power is very similar to the WORDNET-based distance metrics, which is due to the fact that BABELNET encompasses WORDNET resources. Interestingly, the surface-level LCS metric exhibits much higher discriminative power vis-a-vis CTV. Numerical overlap features seems to be least 'attractive' in this comparison, most likely due to the fact that a large fraction of event template pairs tagged as related do not refer to same events but rather different events linked through the same cause or being in some other type of dependency, and thus, more likely reporting on different numerical values. Nevertheless, we hypothesize that exploitation of numerical overlap metrics might come in handy in case of natural and man-made disaster events, which, unfortunately constitute only a small fraction of all events in our corpora.

4.3 Experiment Setup

Experiments were carried out using five different ML models, namely: SVM, Stochastic gradient descent classifier (regularized linear model learned), Decision Tree, Random Forest and AdaBoost classifier. All models were implemented using (Scikit-learn, 2011). Hyper-parameters of each model were tuned using grid search. Each model was trained using full set of event similarity metrics as features[9] and on a subset

---

[9] As regards $WSWO$ metric family we finally considered only $WSWO - Path$ and $WSWO - WP$ variants based on some empirical observations which revealed that the other variant produce very similar scores

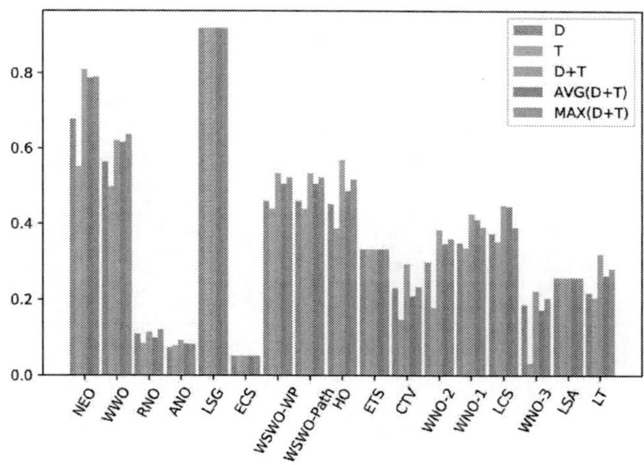

Figure 3: Discriminative power of the event similarity metrics.

of features obtained using feature selection *SelectFromModel* with base estimator being Random Forest. All models consistently exhibited better performance when using all features vis-a-vis subset of features obtained through feature selection. All models were trained on the same train-test split (80:20) and 5-fold cross-validation was performed.

Noteworthy, in case of 'missing' features, i.e., whenever event metric could not be computed (e.g., due to missing elements such as named entities or numerical expressions to be compared), we set the respective values to the mean in the corresponding feature distribution assuming that lack of elements to compare should be scored higher than "zero" overlap (e.g., different named entities in both texts).

Finally, we carried out the evaluation on both datasets described in 4.1 in two set-ups, one with text-based features only, and second one with both textual and meta-data features.

4.4 Results

The performance of the models on GOLD and SILVER datasets is shown in Table 2. The observed results indicate that the task is well modeled by the different classification paradigms, with a Random Forest being in general the top scoring model across all settings. We have also trained additional models using the Random Forest paradigm using subsets of the text-based features set by excluding in each run a single feature in order to explore how the exclusion of each feature impacts the performance. The resulting significance order of the features matches to a larger extent the discriminative power ranking depicted in Figure 3, i.e., NEO, WWO topping the rankings, and ANO and RNO ranking lowest.

As expected (see 4.2) adding meta-data features (in particular given the discriminatory power of LSG) on top of the text-based features significantly boosts the performance, raising the upper bound from 94.7% (92.9% - SILVER) to as much as 98.6% (97% - SILVER). Nevertheless, this is a remarkable finding considering that the meta-data features (i.e., the slots LOCATION, TYPE and CATEGORY) are automatically generated by an event extraction engine and their extraction is more error prone vis-a-vis computation of similarity metrics on the textual slots. One needs to emphasize in this context that the surprisingly high discriminative power of LSG metric that contributed to the overall performance might have been potentially due to the way how the evaluation corpora were built (see Section 4.1).

Moreover, D+T mode seems to be the best choice overall as regards the various modes for computing text-based features and is statistically different with $p < 0.05$ compared to other modes on GOLD dataset with only textual features. Exploiting only title information (T mode) when using text-based features resulted in achieving a respectable F1 score of 84.4% (GOLD) and 80.7% (SILVER).

A rudimentary error analysis on the output of GOLD dataset-trained Random Forest classifier with meta-data features and D+T option revealed that most of the false negatives consisted of event pairs referring to different, related aspects of the same target event, like in the article titles in Figure 4 (top). This was expected as the text pairs have little lexical overlapping and (more) background knowledge (e.g.

ML Paradigm	Text and Meta-data features					Text-based features				
	D	T	D+T	AVG(D,T)	MAX(D,T)	D	T	D+T	AVG(D,T)	MAX(D,T)
SVM	97.39%	97.17%	97.98%	97.66%	97.66%	86.22%	75.20%	93.90%	92.01%	92.24%
SDG	97.42%	97.37%	97.27%	97.83%	97.88%	85.20%	76.11%	93.53%	90.99%	91.80%
RANDOM FOREST	**98.38%**	**98.54%**	**98.57%**	**98.43%**	**98.49%**	**88.69%**	**84.40%**	**94.71%**	**93.62%**	**93.61%**
DECISION TREE	97.92%	97.87%	98.06%	98.18%	98.16%	86.36%	78.93%	94.32%	92.73%	92.99%
ADABOOST	97.85%	97.67%	98.09%	98.04%	98.02%	87.19%	79.68%	93.94%	92.31%	92.55%

ML Paradigm	Text and Meta-data features					Text-based features				
	D	T	D+T	AVG(D,T)	MAX(D,T)	D	T	D+T	AVG(D,T)	MAX(D,T)
SVM	95.78%	95.47%	96.62%	96.07%	96.22%	83.40%	73.02%	91.17%	88.71%	88.93%
SDG	96.08%	95.78%	96.68%	96.28%	96.25%	82.99%	73.26%	90.42%	87.61%	88.54%
RANDOM FOREST	**96.76%**	**96.80%**	**97.01%**	**96.96%**	**96.87%**	**85.39%**	**80.74%**	**92.89%**	**91.42%**	**91.60%**
DECISION TREE	96.23%	96.50%	96.50%	96.21%	96.41%	83.70%	76.39%	92.05%	90.66%	90.59%
ADABOOST	95.96%	96.27%	96.27%	96.06%	96.20%	83.63%	75.22%	91.28%	89.98%	89.84%

Table 2: Performance on the GOLD (top) and SILVER (bottom) dataset (F1 scores).

TITLE: *Concert bomber targeted children*
DESCRIPTION: *British Prime Minister Theresa May said police know the identity of the bomber, who died in the blast late Monday, and believed he acted alone.[...]*

TITLE: *Miley Cyrus 'more cautious' after terror attack at Ariana Grande's gig*
DESCRIPTION: *Miley Cyrus says the terror attack at Ariana Grande's concert has made her "more cautious". A bomb was detonated after Ariana's gig at Manchester Arena earlier this week, leaving 22 people dead and over 50 injured and Miley, 24, admitted it has affected [...]*

TITLE: *Ex-Qaeda affiliate leaders among 25 dead in Syria strike*
DESCRIPTION: *An air strike in Syria on Tuesday killed at least 25 members of former Al-Qaeda affiliate Fateh al-Sham Front including senior figures, a monitor said. Unidentified aircraft hit one of the groups most important bases in Syria, in the northwestern province of Idlib, Syrian Observatory for Human Rights director Rami Abdel Rahman told AFP.*

TITLE: *Syrian air strikes kill at least six civilians*
DESCRIPTION: *ALEPPO - Syrian government air strikes killed at least six civilians, including four children, in Aleppo province on Thursday, despite a fragile two-week-old truce, a monitor said. In neighbouring Idlib province, at least 22 jihadists were killed in air strikes over the past 24 hours, the Syrian Observatory for Human Rights said.*

Figure 4: A sample false negative (top) and false positive (bottom) event pair.

access to full news articles) is required in order to draw a relatedness link. On the other hand, the models struggled to set apart individual incidents (see Figure 4 - bottom) belonging to a larger event context, which typically share lexical profile, LOCATION and TYPE slots. Among all false classifications 60% were false negatives and 40% were false positives.

5 Conclusions

This paper reported one experiments of testing ML methods using a wide range of textual and meta-data features to train classifiers for linking related event templates that have been automatically extracted from online news. While exploiting solely textual features resulted in achieving 94.7% F1 score, adding meta-data features allowed to improve it up to 98.6%, mainly thanks to exploitation of an event similarity metric that computes geographical distance between events with high discriminatory power.

Future research envisaged encompasses: (a) adaptation and evaluation of the approach on event data in other languages, (b) consideration of additional lightweight features (e.g., exploitation of country/region size assuming that events occurring in bigger countries are less likely to be related, utilization of the structure of the urls to the related sources which might hint at reporting over time on some bigger events/stories over certain period of time.), (c) based on the work carried out elaboration of additional event similarity metrics to train models for cross-lingual event linking (Rupnik et al., 2017; Al-Badrashiny et al., 2017), and (d) introducing an additional sub-classification of the 'related' class. As a matter of fact we carried out an initial attempt to sub-classify a sample of 150 event pairs (e_1, e_2) labelled as related into one of the four sub-classes: IDENTITY (reporting on the same event), SAME_CAUSE (e_1 and e_2 were triggered by the same event, e.g., arrests/investigations and visit of a political leader, both following a terrorist attack), e_1 UPDATES_OR_DEPENDS_ON e_2 and the symmetric case (terrorist attack followed by an introduction of an emergency situation). However, the bilateral κ scores between 3 annotators involved ranged from 0.45 to 0.63 which indicates the complexity of the task.

All the resources used in the experiments, i.e., the annotated corpora, files with event similarity metric values in ARFF format and feature histograms can be accessed at: `http://labs.emm4u.eu/eventlinking/event-linking_version_1.0_29.06.2018.zip`.

References

Mohamed Al-Badrashiny, Jason Bolton, Arun Tejasvi Chaganty, Kevin Clark, Craig Harman, Lifu Huang, Matthew Lamm, Jinhao Lei, Di Lu, Xiaoman Pan, Ashwin Paranjape, Ellie Pavlick, Haoruo Peng, Peng Qi, Pushpendre Rastogi, Abigail See, Kai Sun, Max Thomas, Chen-Tse Tsai, Hao Wu, Boliang Zhang, Chris Callison-Burch, Claire Cardie, Heng Ji, Christopher D. Manning, Smaranda Muresan, Owen Rambow, Dan Roth, Mark Sammons, and Benjamin Van Durme. 2017. TinkerBell: Cross-lingual Cold-Start Knowledge Base Construction, *Proceedings of the 2017 Text Analysis Conference, TAC 2017*, 59–65.

Martin Atkinson, Jakub Piskorski, Hristo Tanev, and Vanni Zavarella. 2017. On the Creation of a Security-Related Event Corpus, *Proceedings of the Events and Stories in the News Workshop*, 59–65.

Satanjeev Banerjee and Ted Pedersen. 2002. An Adapted Lesk Algorithm for Word Sense Disambiguation Using WordNet, *Proceedings of the Third International Conference on Computational Linguistics and Intelligent Text Processing*, 136–145.

Cosmin Adrian Bejan and Sanda Harabagiu. 2010. Unsupervised event coreference resolution with rich linguistic features, *Proceedings of the 48th Annual Meeting of the Association for Computational Linguistics*, 1412–1422.

Evgenia Belyaeva, Aljaž Košmerlj, Andrej Muhič, Jan Rupnik, and Flavio Fuart. 2015. Using semantic data to improve cross-lingual linking of article clusters, *Web Semantics: Science, Services and Agents on the World Wide Web*, 35:64–70.

Alexander Budanitsky and Graeme Hirst. 2001. Semantic distance in WordNet: An experimental, application-oriented evaluation of five measures, *Proceedings of NAACL 2001 Workshop on Wordnet and Other Lexical Resources*.

Tommaso Caselli and Piek Vossen. 2017. The Event StoryLine Corpus: A New Benchmark for Causal and Temporal Relation Extraction, *Proceedings of the Events and Stories in the News 2017 Workshop*.

Sophie Chesney, Guillaume Jacquet, Ralf Steinberger, and Jakub Piskorski. 2017. Multi-word Entity Classification in a Highly Multilingual Environment, *Proceedings of the 13th Workshop on Multiword Expressions (MWE 2017)*, 11–20.

Maud Ehrmann, Guillaume Jacquet and Ralf Steinberger. 2017. JRC-Names: Multilingual entity name variants and titles as Linked Data, *Semantic Web*, 8(2):283–295.

Weiwei Guo, Hao Li, Heng Ji, and Mona Diab. 2013. Linking Tweets to News: A Framework to Enrich Short Text Data in Social Media *Proceedings of ACL 2013 - 51st Annual Meeting of the Association for Computational Linguistics*

Gary King and Will Lowe. 2017. An Automated Information Extraction Tool For International Conflict Data with Performance as Good as Human Coders, *International Organization*, 57:617-642.

Sebastian Krause, Feiyu Xu, Hans Uszkoreit, and Dirk Weissenborn. 2016. Event Linking with Sentential Features from Convolutional Neural Networks, *Proceedings of CoNLL 2016*, 239–249.

Quoc Le and Tomas Mikolov. 2014. Distributed Representations of Sentences and Documents, *Proceedings of the 31st International Conference on International Conference on Machine Learning - Volume 32*.

Vladimir Levenshtein. 1965. Binary codes for correcting deletions, insertions, and reversals, *Doklady Akademii Nauk SSSR*, 163(4):845–848.

Teruko Mitamura, Zhengzhong Liu, and Eduard Hovy. 2015. Overview of TAC KBP 2015 Event Nugget Track, *Text Analysis Conference*.

Gonzalo Navarro. 2001. A guided tour to approximate string matching, *ACM Comput. Surv.*, 33(1):31–88.

Roberto Navigli and Simone Paolo Ponzetto. 2012. BabelNet: The Automatic Construction, Evaluation and Application of a Wide-Coverage Multilingual Semantic Network, *Artificial Intelligence*, 193:217–250.

Joel Nothman, Matthew Honnibal, Ben Hachey, and James R. Curran. 2012. Event Linking: Grounding Event Reference in a News Archive, *Proceedings of ACL 2012*.

Jeffrey Pennington, Richard Socher, and Christopher D. Manning. 2014. GloVe: Global Vectors for Word Representation, *Proceedings of Empirical Methods in Natural Language Processing 2014*, 1532–1543.

Jakub Piskorski, Karol Wieloch, and Marcin Sydow. 2009. On knowledge-poor methods for person name matching and lemmatization for highly inflectional languages, *Information Retrieval*, 12(3):275–299.

Jan Rupnik, Andrej Muhič, Gregor Leban, Blaz Fortuna, and Marko Grobelnik. 2017. News Across Languages: Cross-lingual Document Similarity and Event Tracking, *Proceedings of the 26th International Joint Conference on Artificial Intelligence (IJCAI 2017)*, 5050–5054.

Frane Šarić, Goran Glavaš, Mladen Karan, Jan Šnajder, and Bojana Dalbelo Bašić. 2012. TakeLab: Systems for Measuring Semantic Text Similarity, *Proceedings of the First Joint Conference on Lexical and Computational Semantics - Volume 1: Proceedings of the Main Conference and the Shared Task, and Volume 2: Proceedings of the Sixth International Workshop on Semantic Evaluation*, 441–448.

F. Pedregosa, G. Varoquaux, A. Gramfort, V. Michel, B. Thirion, O. Grisel, M. Blondel, P. Prettenhofer, R. Weiss, V. Dubourg, J. Vanderplas, A. Passos, D. Cournapeau, M. Brucher, M. Perrot, and E. Duchesnay, "Scikit-learn: Machine learning in Python," *Journal of Machine Learning Research*, vol. 12, pp. 2825–2830, 2011.

Richard Socher, Eric H. Huang, Jeffrey Pennington, Andrew Y. Ng, and Christopher D. Manning. 2011. Dynamic Pooling and Unfolding Recursive Autoencoders for Paraphrase Detection, *Proceedings of the 24th International Conference on Neural Information Processing Systems (NIPS 2011)*, 801–809.

Piek Vossen, Rodrigo Agerri, Itziar Aldabe, Agata Cybulska, Marieke van Erp, Antske Fokkens, Egoitz Laparra, Anne-Lyse Minard, Alessio Palmero Aprosio, German Rigau, Marco Rospocher, and Roxane Segers. 2016. NewsReader: Using knowledge resources in a cross-lingual reading machine to generate more knowledge from massive streams of news, *Knowledge-Based Systems*, 110:60–85.

Zhibiao Wu and Marta Palmer. 1994. Verbs Semantics and Lexical Selection, *Proceedings of ACL 1994 - 32nd Annual Meeting on Association for Computational Linguistics*, 133–138.

Roman Yangarber, Peter Von Etter, and Ralf Steinberger. 2008. Content Collection and Analysis in the Domain of Epidemiology, *Proceedings of DrMED 2008: International Workshop on Describing Medical Web Resources at MIE 2008: the 21st International Congress of the European Federation for Medical Informatics 2008*.

HEI: Hunter Events Interface
A platform based on services for the detection and reasoning about events

Antonio Sorgente, Antonio Calabrese, Gianluca Coda, Paolo Vanacore and Francesco Mele
Institute of Applied Sciences and Intelligent Systems "Eduardo Caianiello"
National Research Council
Via Campi Flegrei 34, 80078 Pozzuoli (Naples) Italy
{a.sorgente, a.calabrese, g.coda, p.vanacore, f.mele}@isasi.cnr.it

Abstract

In this paper we present the definition and implementation of the Hunter Events Interface (HEI) System. The HEI System is a system for events annotation and temporal reasoning in Natural Language Texts and media, mainly oriented to texts of historical and cultural contents available on the Web. In this work we assume that events are defined through various components: actions, participants, locations, and occurrence intervals. The HEI system, through independent services, locates (annotates) the various components, and successively associates them to a specific event. The objective of this work is to build a system integrating services for the identification of events, the discovery of their connections, and the evaluation of their consistency. We believe this interface is useful to develop applications that use the notion of story, to integrate data of digital cultural archives, and to build systems of fruition in the same field. The HEI system has been partially developed within the TrasTest project [1].

1 Introduction

The amount of digital resources is growing day by day, and this raises new challenges in the management process in particular in the access and reuse of such resources. For this aim we need systems that offer solutions to effectively store digital resources (text, images, video, etc.) and allow us to give them an interpretation with respect to a given semantic.

Our contribution in this direction regards the definition and implementation of a system that permits a user to manage resources (mainly textual resources, but also media resource) and easily annotate them. We called this system HEI (Hunter Events Interface).

Today in research areas of Natural Language (NL) and temporal reasoning there are numerous tools that help NL text analysis and facilitate applications in many different sectors. Many research groups have made available on the Web some of their own developed tools (parsers, name detectors, etc ..) providing, in particular in the field of temporal representation and reasoning, a little support for the integration of such services. This work is born with the goal of developing a methodology that integrates services concerning annotation, discovery, connectivity, and temporal reasoning through events in natural language texts provided by different developers and also, offering services to annotate media. Through the use of such annotations, we can define multimedia streams that coherently synchronises media elements with a synthetic voice delivering the textual content, and retrieve information to respond to queries as in dialog systems.

For the annotation of natural language texts we have chosen CSWL (Cultural Story Web Language) as referred semantic formalism, and according to CSWL we have established the following annotation approach, that can be made by the particular HEI architecture:

1. for each text in NL, it applies n basic services Sn automatically annotating the text with significant labels for the CSWL semantics (basic services Sn are available in Web or are part of an internal repository HEI) producing m annotated entities (see section 4.1);

---

[1] TrasTest (Transforming Texts on Cultural Knowledge in Structured Data) is a project of National Research Council (CNR)

Proceedings of the Workshop on Events and Stories in the News, pages 79–88
Santa Fe, New Mexico, USA, August 20, 2018.

2. some services (algorithms on temporal grammatical, semantic or pragmatic properties emerging from the NL text) are applied to extend the m entity previously annotated (see section 4.2);

3. we can monitor the made annotations, and interactively execute the completion of annotations.

In literature there are some systems that allow browsing and text annotation (Hou et al., 2015; de Boer et al., 2015; Vossen et al., 2016). In (Hou et al., 2015; Vossen et al., 2016) the authors presented NewsMiner and NewsReader system respectively, and both are focused on the interpretation of news using an event-based formalism. In (de Boer et al., 2015), in particular, the focus is on historical events. Our system is also based on an event formalism, but in addition to events takes into account fluents and complex events. Moreover HEI system allows users to evaluate the temporal consistency of text, and can be expanded with the addition of new annotation services.

In this paper we introduce the CSWL formalism (section 2), the architecture of the HEI system (section 3) and some services implemented in the system (section 4).

2 CSWL Formalism

CSWL (Cultural Story Web Language) is a formalism based on a cognitive notion of event, based on five "Ws" (Who, What, Where, When and Why) (Sorgente et al., 2016a; Mele and Sorgente, 2015). We consider an event as an action that happens over time that has participants and a location where it takes place. Differently from other event-based formalism (such as those defined in (van Hage et al., 2011; Wang et al., 2007; Scherp et al., 2009)), through CSWL formalism we can also represent the major entities that change over time: properties of event participants, spatial and meronomic relations of objects composing the architectural structures, and function of artifacts. We represent such entities as fluents, the same concept defined in the Event Calculus (Mueller, 2015). In the same way, in CSWL social roles of people (or historical characters) are entities that change over time, and are represented as relationships representing capabilities to perform potential actions. We have inserted in the formalism primitives to represent emotional roles owned by artworks in relation to their shapes and colours. With CSWL we can represent complex events as single units (aggregations of more events), having each a name and properties set. In CWSL, stories are complex events represented by a set of events having causal (and therefore temporal) relations between them. In CSWL formalism we can represent concepts based on events through classes, on which we can associate (and apply) inference rules. All the entities that change over time – the properties, roles, spatial relationships, and mental attitudes of the characters – are grouped together in CSWL in a same class (fluent), and rules for the reasoning on persistence and change of properties over time, are applied uniformly to each element of such class.

We report in the form of first order logic relations, the main classes of CSWL. In the ontological formulation of CSWL, there are three basic entities:

- events (simple) - are entities that happen on a time interval;
- fluents - are entities that change over time, they are true (or false) at specific instants (or time intervals), can cease or start to be true again;
- complex events - are aggregations of simple events or other complex events

```
% AnythingInTime Taxonomy
anythingInTime(X):-event(X). anythingInTime(X):-complexEvent(X).
anythingInTime(X):-fluent(X).
%Same categories of events
event(X):-reportingThingEvent(X). event(X):-state(X).
event(X):-occurrence(X).      event(X):-perceptionThingEvent(X).
%Event --- Definition Scheme
event(Ex):- hasWhen(Ex,Wnx), hasWhat(Ex,Wtx), hasWhere(Ex,Wrx),
   hasWho(Ex,Wox), wtRel(Wtx), woRel(Wox), wrRel(Wrx), whRel(Wnx).
whRel(Wnx):- has(Wnx,Tmodx), has(Tmodx,Intx), tmod(Tmodx), int(Intx).
tmod(Tmodx):-on(Tmodx). tmod(Tmodx):-after(Tmodx). tmod(Tmodx):-prec(Tmodx).
tmod(Tmodx):-in(Tmodx). tmod(Tmodx):-finish(Tmodx). tmod(Tmodx):-start(Tmodx).
%Complex event --- scheme definition
complexEvent(Cex):- hasWhenC(Cex,Cwn), hasWhatC(Cex,Cwt),
               hasWhereC(Cex,Cwr), hasWhoC(Cex,Cwo).
%Property Fluent -- scheme definition
```

```prolog
fluent(F):- hasWhenF(F, WhenF), hasWhatF(F, WhatF),
          relWhenF(WhenF), relWhatF(WhatF).
relWhenF(WhenF):-temporalTerm(WhenF).
relWhenF(WhenF):-int(WhenF). relWhenF(WhenF):-after(WhenF).
relWhenF(WhenF):-prec(WhenF). relWhenF(WhenF):-finish(WhenF).
relWhenF(WhenF):-start(WhenF). relWhenF(WhenF):-in(WhenF).
relWhat(WhatF):-property(WhatF). relWhat(WhatF):-role(WhatF).
relWhat(WhatF):-mentalAct(WhatF). relWhat(WhatF):-partPartWhoRel(WhatF).
relWhat(WhatF):-spatialRelation(WhatF).
relWhat(WhatF):-emotionalFunction(WhatF). relWhat(WhatF):-artFunction(WhatF).
role(WhatF):-socialRole(WhatF).
%Property -- scheme definition
property(Propx):- hasPrName(Propx, Pnamex),
   hasPrSubject(Propx, Subjx), hasPrValue(Propx, Valuex).
%Role - definition
role(Rox):- hasName(Rox, RoleNamex),
   hasRoParticipant1(Rox, Px1), hasRoParticipant2(Rox, Px2).
%Mental Act
mentalAct(Mactx):- hasMentalAtt(Mactx,Mattx), hasAgent(Mattx,Agx),
   hasEvent(Mattx,Ex), mentalAtt(Mattx), event(Ex), agent(Agx).
% Types of Mental Attitudes
mentalAtt(X):-believe(X). mentalAtt(X):-intention(X). mentalAtt(X):-desire(X).
%Meronomic Relation
partPartWhoRel(PartWhoRelx):- hasType(PartWhoRelx,TypeRelPx),
   hasPart(TypeRelPx,Partx), hasWhole(TypeRelPx, Wholex), typeRelPt(TypeRelPx).
% Types of Meronomic Relations
typeRelPt(X):-relPtCo(X). % Component-Object.
typeRelPt(X):-relPtMc(X). % Member - Collection.
typeRelPm(X):-relPtMc(X). % Portion - Mass.
typeRelMo(X):-relPtMc(X). % Material - Object.
typeRelCa(X):-relPtMc(X). % Feature - Activity.
typeRelSa(X):-relPtMc(X). % Site - Area.
%A taxonomy of Spatial Relations
spatialRelationType(Sr):-qualitativeRel(Sr).
spatialRelationType(Sr):-quantitativeRel(Sr).
quantitativeRel(Sr):- polar(Sr). quantitativeRel(Sr):- logitudinal(Sr).
quantitativeRel(Sr):-cartesian(Sr). qualitativeRel(Sr):-directional(Sr).
qualitativeRel(Sr):- proximity(Sr). qualitativeRel(Sr):- topological(Sr).
topological(Sr):- contains(Sr). topological(Sr):- covers(Sr).
topological(Sr):- meets(Sr). topological(Sr):- overlying(Sr).
topological(Sr):- covered(Sr). topological(Sr):- overlap(Sr).
directional(Sr):- over(Sr). directional(Sr):- high(Sr).
directional(Sr):- under(Sr). directional(Sr):- cardinal(Sr).
directional(Sr):- low(Sr). directional(Sr):- right(Sr).
directional(Sr):- left(Sr). cardinal(Sr):- east(Sr).
cardinal(Sr):- south(Sr). cardinal(Sr):- north(Sr). cardinal(Sr):- west(Sr).
%Social Role
socialRole(RolRelx):- hasName(RolRelx,Namex), hasRoParticipant1(RolRelx, Wo1),
   hasRoParticipant2(RolRelx, Wo2), hasCapability(Wo1,Canx),
   capability(Canx), participant(Wo1), participant(Wo2).
capability(Canx):- hasAction(Canx,Actionx), action(Actionx).
%Artifact Function
artificat(Artx):- hasStructur(Artx,Strx), hasFunction(Artx,Funx),
   hasBehavior(Artx,Behx), artStructur(Strx),
   artFunction(Funx), artBehavior(Behx).
artStructur(Strx):- hasSpatialRelation(Strx,Relx), spatialRelation(Relx).
spatialRelation(Relx):- hasType(Relx,TypeRelPx),spatialRelationType(TypeRelPx),
   hasComponent1(Relx, C1), hasComponent2(Relx, C2),
   artifactPart(C1), artifactPart(C2).
artFunction(Funx):-
   hasName(Funx,Namex), hasCapability(Funx,Canx), capability(Canx).
artBehavior(Behx):- hasName(Behx,Namex), hasStimulus(Behx ,Stimulusx),
   hasEffect(Behx,Effectx), cause(Stimulusx, Effectx),
   event(Stimulusx), event(Effectx).
%Emotional Function
emotionalFunction(EmRelx):- hasName(EmRelx,Namex), hasEmObject(EmRelx, Objx),
   hasEmParticipant(EmRelx, Wox), hasCapabilityEm(Objx,Canx), capabilityEm(Canx),
   participant(Objx),participant(Wox).
addEmot(bel(Wox, Emotionx)):- visuaAct(Wox,Objx), emotionalFunction(EmRelx),
   hasEmObject(EmRelx, Objx), hasEmParticipant(EmRelx, Wox), emotion(Emotionx).
%A taxonomy for Natural Entities
naturalEntity(X):-socialAgent(X). naturalEntity(X):-naturalPhenomenon(X).
naturalEntity(X):-physicalAgent(X). naturalEntity(X):-physicalObject(X).
physicalAgent(X):-person(X).  physicalAgent(X):-animal(X).
socialAgent(X):-groupAgent(X). socialAgent(X):-collectiveAgent(X).
physicalObject(X):-media(X).  physicalObject(X):-artifactPart(X).
%Temporal expression classes
```

```
temporalExp(X):-interval(X).  temporalExp(X):-temporalTerm(X).
temporalTerm(X):-dataValue(X). temporalTerm(X):-timeValue(X).
dataValue(X):-dateCalendar(X). dataValue(X):-dateWeek(X).
dataValue(X):-dataQualitative(X). timeValue(X):-timeQualitative(X).
timeValue(X):-clock(X).
% Definitions for the temporal taxonomy
clock(Clx):-
    hasHour(Clx, Hourx), hasMinute(Clx, Minutex), hasSecond(Clx, Secondx).
date(Dcx):- hasYear(Dcx, Yearx), hasMonth(Dcx, Monthx), hasDay(Dcx, Dayx).
dataCalendar(Dayx,Monthx,Yearx):- date(Dcx), hasYear(Dcx, Yearx),
    hasMonth(Dcx, Monthx), hasDay(Dcx, Dayx).
dateWeek(Dwx):- hasMonth(Dwx, Monthx), hasDay(Dwx, Dayx).
dateWeekCalendar(Monthx,Dayx):-
    dateWeek(Dwx), hasMonth(Dwx, Monthx), hasDay(Dwx, Dayx).
interval(Intx):-
    begin(Intx,Tt1), end(Intx, Tt2), temporalTerm(Tt1), temporalTerm(Tt2).
dataQualitative(Dq) :- hasTimeQualitative(Dq,Tq),
    convertFunction(Tq,Datax), timeQualitative(Tq), dataValue(Datax).
timeQualitative(Tq) :- annotation(Tkx, Tq), token(Tkx).
```

3   Architecture

The HEI [2] (Hunter Events Interface) system consists of software modules which assist the user in the semantic annotation process of NL texts and multimedia containing events. The HEI framework is based on a plugin architecture, so the system is modular and easily extendable. The plugin architecture (Fig. 1) allows us to extend the tool functionalities with respect to the format of the reference ontology, automatic annotation, reasoning on events, annotation and semantic multimedia mashup export. All the services shown below permit users to annotate automatically the text, but also, through the interface they can modify, add or remove the annotations.

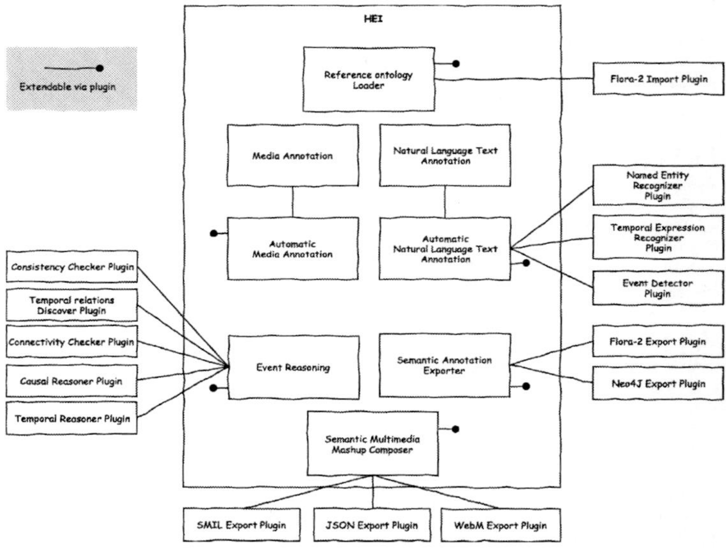

Figure 1: HEI Architecture diagram

The particular architecture of HEI allows us to use different reference ontologies for the semantic annotation, and, through its *import plugins*, the system is able to import ontologies, written in different formalism. About this, we have developed a specific plugin "F2ImportPlugin" to load reference ontologies written in Flora-2[3].

In Fig. 2 a screen-shot of HEI interface is reported. On the left of the screen there is the reference ontology used to annotate the text, the latter is shown in the centre of the screen. The user selects the

[2]http://smcm.isasi.cnr.it/lab/hei-hunter-of-event-interface/

[3]http://flora.sourceforge.net/

class to be instantiated, from the left column, he can select the text to annotate, and in the bottom of the screen can see the instance attributes filled. On the right side of screen, the ontology instances are shown.

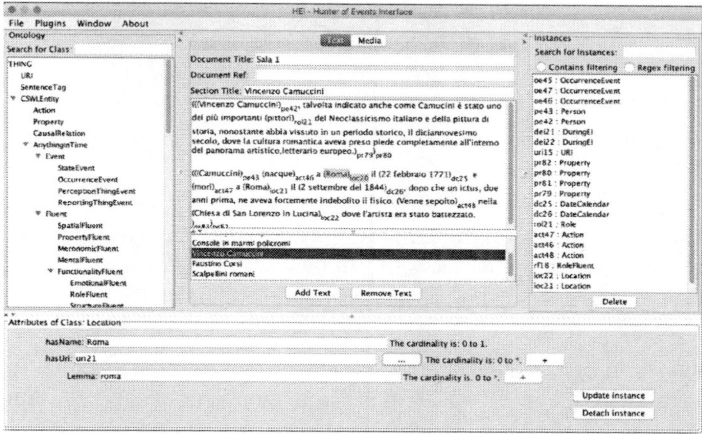

Figure 2: HEI Annotation GUI

The main aim of HEI is to have an environment that permits in automatic or assisted way, the annotation of temporal entities, and the analysation of the text on such annotations. For this reason a set of plugins has been built. Given a text in NL, with the HEI interface we access to the "*Plugins → Auto − Annotation*" menu (Fig. 3a), and can launch the plugins for automatic text annotation (Fig. 3b).

Developed plugins are based on services described in 4.1. We have implemented: "DandelionPlugin" for name entity recognition using the Dandelion API[4] to detect the participants in events; "EventDetectorPlugin" for detecting events; and "TemporalExpressionPlugin" using HeidelTime(Strötgen and Gertz, 2015), for annotating temporal expressions. Plugins architecture of the HEI system adopts the approach described in (Vanacore et al., 2016), where a method for defining mapping between different representations has been presented. In order to match instances of the representation models adopted by the auto-annotation services, with the reference ontology used for the annotation, we use an interface for executing the mapping among different representations. For this aim we use some bridge rules allowing the semantic linking of the entities (see Fig. 4.)

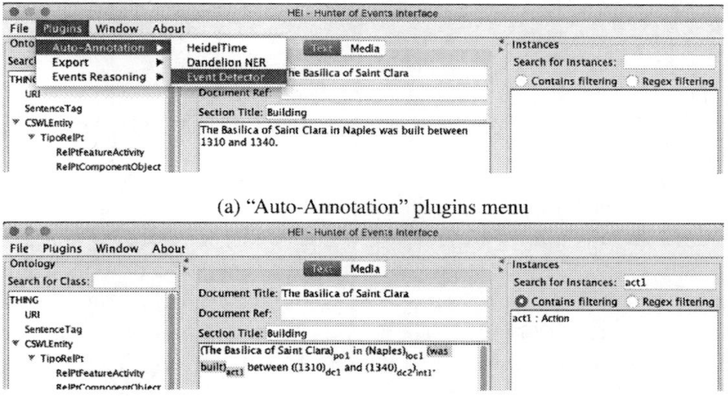

(a) "Auto-Annotation" plugins menu

(b) example of automatic detected events by the "EventDetector" plugin

Figure 3: HEI Annotation GUI

---

[4]https://dandelion.eu

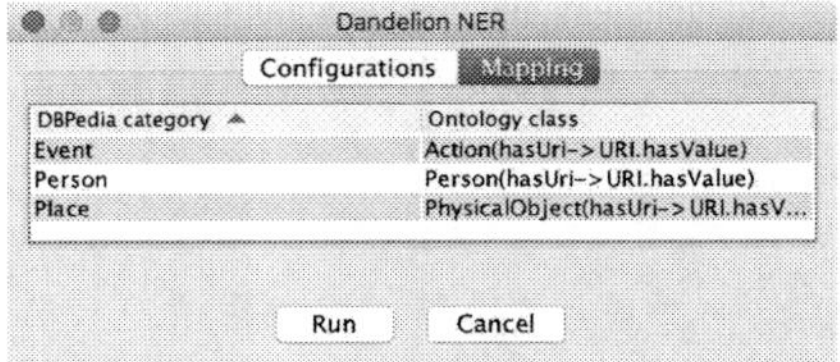

Figure 4: HEI GUI - Example of mapping rules for the Dandelion NER service

The HEI architecture allows us to add reasoning services, mapping concepts present in referring ontology with the schema adopted by the reasoner. In this case, after the process of annotation, the user can run reasoning services using the implemented mapping. At this time of HEI system development are present various services for events reasoning.

To store the annotation, we developed some plugins for annotations export: "F2Export Plugin" to export annotations in Flora-2, and "NEO4JExportPlugin" to export annotations into Neo4J[5] graph. In Fig. 5 we report a screenshot of a Neo4J graph, obtained by the "NEO4JExportPlugin", with 4860 nodes and 7468 relationships.

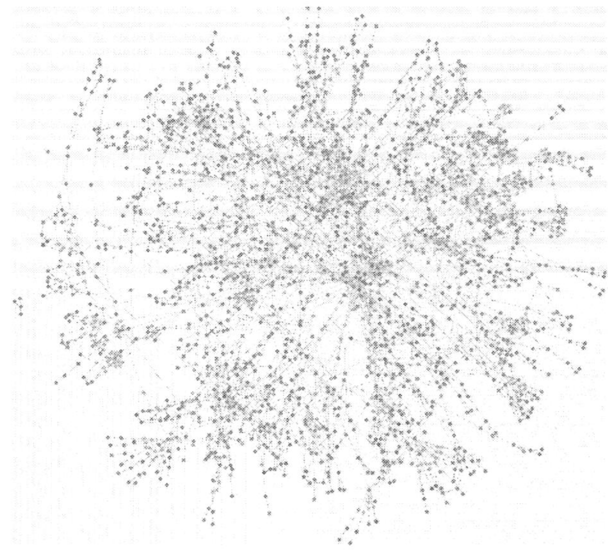

Figure 5: Example of Neo4J graph obtained with the "NEO4JExportPlugin"

Through HEI we can semantically annotate the media (Fig. 6). The annotator can adds video or images, specifying a remote Uniform Resource Locator (URL), or selecting a file from the local filesystem. The annotations can be associated to a text related to the media or to the media directly. Having different resource types annotated with the same semantic, we can define services that permit building of artefacts by composing such resources. Through this annotation, it is possible produce multimedia presentations that synchronise text, images and video in a unique stream. Developed plugins can export multimedia artefacts in SMIL[6] JSON and Webm[7] formats. An application of such services was presented in (Sorgente et al., 2016b)

---

[5]https://neo4j.com/
[6]https://www.w3.org/TR/SMIL/
[7]http://www.webmproject.org/

Figure 6: HEI Media Annotation GUI

4 Services

The CSWL formalism represents historical entities through classes of an ontology. This permits us to facilitate the automatic annotation processes, the reuse of the existing axiomatics in the research of temporal reasoning and the creation of new ones. In this section we present the HEI framework services for texts analysis. Some basic services regard the annotation process, they are used to identify the concepts inside the text and to represent them through the formalism defined in section 2, while other services of temporal reasoning extract new relations among temporal entities.

4.1 Annotation services

The services used in the HEI framework are known in the literature (such as Danedelion, HeidelTime) and services defined by us (such as EventDetection, TempRel).

Named Entity Recognition. Named Entity Recognition (NER) is a service that recognises locations, persons, and other entities inside the text. We have implemented NER plugin that uses Dandelion, a set of services offered by Spaziodati[8]. NER provides as output a set of expressions with associated semantic information. Often, some results do not have any associated semantic label, Dandelion API classifies them as a generic concept. For these reasons in HEI exists a taxonomy of lexical terms for cultural heritage domain that allows us to associate the right category to art objects: painting, sculpture etc..

Temporal Expression Recognition. Temporal Expression Recognition (TER) is a service that recognises temporal expressions in the text. For the implementation of *TER plugin* we have used Heidel-Time (Strötgen and Gertz, 2015) that is a "multilingual, domain-sensitive temporal tagger" developed at the Database Systems Research Group at Heidelberg University. The service annotates temporal expressions, such as times, dates, durations, etc., in NL texts and normalises them according to the TIMEX3 tag defined in the TimeML Specification[9]. HeidelTime is based on hand-crafted resources for 13 languages, and starting from the version 2.0, contains automatically generated resources for over 200 languages. For each language HeidelTime is able to distinguish between news and narrative document types, in particular for English only, colloquial documents and scientific articles are also supported. The output formats of the service are TimeML and XMI.

Temporal Relation. The service allows us to annotate temporal relationships between events and temporal expressions within a text. For this purpose, besides the text, the service requires that events and temporal expressions have already been annotated. The latter are provided by HeidelTime and Event-Detector. The temporal relation service is based on rules defined on the dependency tree. Given two entities (events and/or temporal expressions), the rules evaluate the syntactic expressions in the text between them. In particular prepositions and adverbs are considered for labelling a specific relationship.

---

[8]http://www.spaziodati.eu/
[9]http://www.timeml.org/publications/timeMLdocs/timeml_1.2.html

The relations considered are those defined in (Allen, 1983): After, During, Start, Meet, etc.. . More details about this service were presented in (Pastore, 2013).

Event-Detector. As presented in section 2, an event is an action that happens over time and involves one or more participants. Starting from this definition, we have an event for each action detected in the text. So we have a service for detecting actions. Such service is defined through a rules-based approach that analyses verbs, nouns, adjectives and adverbs in the text and decides if an expression is an action or not (more details about this service were presented at (Cisternino, 2013)). After the detection of the actions, and knowing the other components (location, temporal expression, agent and physical objects) detected with previous services, the aim is to compose the events associating actions with other components. The composition process is still in the phase of completion and evaluation, but principally, it is based on the analysis of the dependency tree and the relationships between the entities and the actions identified in the text.

Media-Annotation. This service annotates the media using CSWL formalism. At this development stage of HEI, the annotation of media is associated to the whole media (not its parts) or to the caption associated to it (Fig. 6).

4.2 Reasoning services

We can apply various services or axiomatics (formalized in terms of logic programming) to NL texts annotated through CSWL formalism. These services concern temporal reasoning about intervals or events, coherence checking of events, discovery of temporal relationships between events, verification of the connectivity of narrative events, causal reasoning through events. Some details of the following services are described in (Mele et al., 2010; Mele and Sorgente, 2011; Mele and Sorgente, 2013).

Consistency check of events. The consistency check of events regards the consistency of temporal relations in which the events are involved. To implement such a service, the axioms of Russell and Kamp (RK) (Van Lambalgen and Hamm, 2008) have been adopted as input for defining the logical rules (in ASP logic program) that allow the detection of subsequent inconsistency. In particular, a logic ASP program using Clingo system(Gebser et al., 2010), has been developed. The program, given a knowledge base defined through the relations between time points, calculates the stable models, or rather, groups of consistent sets of relations (satisfying the RK axioms). If the program returns more than one stable model, then the relations are inconsistent. Each stable model will contain all consistent relations, if it returns a unique stable model, meaning that the relations between events are consistent.

Discovery of temporal relations among events. The aim of this service is to enrich the set of temporal relations between events. The starting point of this reasoner is to detect a consistent set of events (checked with previous service). Then, once the consistency of temporal relationships has been provided and the only possible stable model (coming from previous service) has been identified, the service identifies new temporal relations between events. For this purpose, a specific set of rules for each temporal relation among events has been defined. Each rule tries to find a particular temporal relationship (before, after, meets, etc.) between two events in accordance with the relations belonging to the stable model returned.

Connectivity check of narrative events. The partial temporal order of events does not ensure that all events belonging to a story are connected. This may be because during the annotation process some relations were not detected and/or because in the text the temporal relations are not present. For this reason, we have implemented a service to evaluate the connectivity of narrative events. The algorithm finds the connected components using a graph representation where the nodes are the events and the edges are the temporal relations between them.

Causal reasoning through events. For causal reasoning service, we have implemented a set of rules (in logic program form) based on the axiomatic defined in (Bochman, 2003)). Through these rules, the system can imply new causal relations, and also provides a consistency check of causal relations. As for the *consistency check of events* service, a logic program through stable model semantics (Gelfond and Lifschitz, 1988) using Clingo system(Gebser et al., 2010), has been implemented.

Persistence fluent reasoner. This set of rules is necessary to evaluate the persistence of all fluent entities present in the CSWL formalism (properties, roles, mental acts, spatial and meronomic relations).

To this end, a service based on Event Calculus has been defined to determine the validity of fluents over time. We have used the *dec.lp* program reported in (Mueller, 2015) and integrated it with others reasoner programs.

Semantic multimedia mashups. A particular aspect concerning this system is the possibility to build *syncretic multimedia artefacts* (Cosenza, 2010; Sorgente et al., 2016a), that semantically synchronise events present in NL texts, extradiegetic voices or captions, with the homologous events present in video annotations. Given a text, this service selects and ranks available media that can be associated to entities annotated in such a text. Both resources, text and media, are annotated by CSWL, so the ranking is based on an index calculated by comparing the CSWL annotation of media with respect to the annotations of the text. It checks if they (media and text) have a common annotation of some entities, that is if the media has annotated entities that are cited in the text. After selecting the media, they are synchronised with synthesised text (through a Text To Speech tool) so that media items are coherently visualised with the relevant time intervals in which a synthetic voice talks about the content represented in the media. An application of such a service has been presented in (Sorgente et al., 2016b).

5 Conclusions

In this work, we have presented the HEI system that helps a user in the annotation of NL text. HEI is composed of various modules, and has as reference ontology CSWL formalism. The HEI architecture is based on services that are implemented as plugins, specialised to execute particular forms of temporal reasoning (named entity recognition, temporal expression recognition, temporal relation extraction, media annotation, consistency check of events, discovery of temporal relations, connectivity check, causal reasoning and persistence fluent reasoning). In HEI there are services for the integration of plugins present in the system. Such a system was used to annotate cultural texts of '800 exhibit at the Capodimonte Museum and to export them as a Neo4j graph (Fig. 5). Based on these annotations, a dialogue system recovering answers for user's queries was defined (Origlia et al., 2016; Sorgente et al., 2016b).

References

James F. Allen. 1983. Maintaining knowledge about temporal intervals. Commun. ACM, 26(11):832–843, November.

Alexander Bochman. 2003. On disjunctive causal inference and indeterminism. In IJCAI Workshop: NRAC-03, pages 45–50.

Alessandra Cisternino. 2013. Un sistema ad approccio linguistico per la scoperta di eventi in testi di linguaggio naturale. Tesi di laurea, Università degli Studi di Napoli "PARTHENOPE".

Giovanna Cosenza. 2010. Semiotica dei nuovi media. Laterza.

Victor de Boer, Johan Oomen, Oana Inel, Lora Aroyo, Elco van Staveren, Werner Helmich, and Dennis de Beurs. 2015. Dive into the event-based browsing of linked historical media. Web Semantics: Science, Services and Agents on the World Wide Web, 35:152 – 158. Semantic Web Challenge 2014.

Martin Gebser, Roland Kaminski, Benjamin Kaufmann, Max Ostrowski, Torsten Schaub, and Sven Thiele. 2010. A users guide to gringo, clasp, clingo, and iclingo.

Michael Gelfond and Vladimir Lifschitz. 1988. The stable model semantics for logic programming. In ICLP/SLP, volume 88, pages 1070–1080.

Lei Hou, Juanzi Li, Zhichun Wang, Jie Tang, Peng Zhang, Ruibing Yang, and Qian Zheng. 2015. Newsminer: Multifaceted news analysis for event search. Knowledge-Based Systems, 76:17 – 29.

Francesco Mele and Antonio Sorgente. 2011. The temporal representation and reasoning of complex events. In CILC, pages 385–399.

Francesco Mele and Antonio Sorgente. 2013. OntotimeFL–a formalism for temporal annotation and reasoning for natural language text. In New Challenges in Distributed Information Filtering and Retrieval, pages 151–170. Springer.

Francesco Mele and Antonio Sorgente. 2015. CSWL - Cultural Stories Web Language. Technical Report 180/15, Institute of Cybernetics "E. Caianiello" of CNR, 06 March.

Francesco Mele, Antonio Sorgente, and Giuseppe Vettigli. 2010. Designing and building multimedia cultural stories using concepts of film theories and logic programming. In AAAI Fall Symposium: Cognitive and Metacognitive Educational Systems.

Erik T Mueller. 2015. Commonsense reasoning: an event calculus based approach. Morgan Kaufmann.

Antonio Origlia, Enrico Leone, Antonio Sorgente, Paolo Vanacore, Maria Parascandolo, Francesco Mele, and Francesco Cutugno. 2016. Designing interactive experiences to explore artwork collections: a multimedia dialogue system supporting visits in museum exhibits. In Proceedings of the 10th AI*IA 2016, volume 1772 of CEUR Workshop Proceedings, pages 26–33. CEUR-WS.org.

Annamaria Pastore. 2013. Un sistema ad approccio linguistico per la scoperta di relazioni temporali in testi di linguaggio naturale. Tesi di laurea, Università degli Studi di Napoli "PARTHENOPE".

Ansgar Scherp, Thomas Franz, Carsten Saathoff, and Steffen Staab. 2009. F–a model of events based on the foundational ontology dolce+dns ultralight. In Proceedings of the Fifth International Conference on Knowledge Capture, K-CAP '09, pages 137–144, New York, NY, USA. ACM.

Antonio Sorgente, Antonio Calabrese, Gianluca Coda, Paolo Vanacore, and Francesco Mele. 2016a. Building multimedial dialogues annotating heterogeneous resources. In Luciana Bordoni, Francesco Mele, and Antonio Sorgente, editors, Artificial Intelligence for Cultural Heritage, chapter 3, pages 49–82. Cambridge Scholars Publishing.

Antonio Sorgente, Paolo Vanacore, Antonio Origlia, Enrico Leone, Francesco Cutugno, and Francesco Mele. 2016b. Multimedia responses in natural language dialogues. In Proceedings of AVI*CH 2016, volume 1621 of CEUR Workshop Proceedings, pages 15–18. CEUR-WS.org.

Jannik Strötgen and Michael Gertz. 2015. A baseline temporal tagger for all languages. In Proceedings of the 2015 Conference on Empirical Methods in Natural Language Processing, pages 541–547, Lisbon, Portugal. Association for Computational Linguistics.

Willem Robert van Hage, Véronique Malaisé, Roxane Segers, Laura Hollink, and Guus Schreiber. 2011. Design and use of the simple event model (SEM). J. Web Sem., 9(2):128–136.

Michiel Van Lambalgen and Fritz Hamm. 2008. The proper treatment of events, volume 6. John Wiley & Sons.

Paolo Vanacore, Gianluca Coda, Antonio Sorgente, and Francesco Mele. 2016. Creazione di servizi intelligenti da implementare su piattaforme gi esistenti. Istituto di Scienze Applicate e Sistemi Intelligenti "Eduardo Caianiello" (ISASI), CNR. Int. Report 182/1615.

Piek Vossen, Rodrigo Agerri, Itziar Aldabe, Agata Cybulska, Marieke van Erp, Antske Fokkens, Egoitz Laparra, Anne-Lyse Minard, Alessio Palmero Aprosio, German Rigau, Marco Rospocher, and Roxane Segers. 2016. Newsreader: Using knowledge resources in a cross-lingual reading machine to generate more knowledge from massive streams of news. Knowledge-Based Systems, 110:60 – 85.

Xiang-jun Wang, Swathi Mamadgi, Atit Thekdi, Aisling Kelliher, and Hari Sundaram. 2007. Eventory – an event based media repository. In Proceedings of the International Conference on Semantic Computing, ICSC '07, pages 95–104, Washington, DC, USA. IEEE Computer Society.

Author Index

Atkinson, Martin, 68

Bonial, Claire, 55

Calabrese, Antonio, 79
Caselli, Tommaso, 44
Coda, Gianluca, 79
Cornelio, Cristina, 25
Croft, William, 7

Dai, Zeyu, 61

Finlayson, Mark, 25

Gao, Tian, 25

Huang, Ruihong, 61

Inel, Oana, 44

Krishnaswamy, Nikhil, 1
Kwon, Heesung, 55

Lee, Sook-kyung, 7

Mele, Francesco, 79
Miller, Ben, 18

Peskova, Pavlina, 7
Piskorski, Jakub, 68
Pustejovsky, James, 1

Reale, Christopher, 55
Regan, Michael, 7

Saric, Fredi, 68
Sorgente, Antonio, 79

Taneja, Himanshu, 61

Vanacore, Paolo, 79
Voss, Clare, 55

Yarlott, W. Victor, 25
Yu, Bei, 34
Yuan, Shi, 34

Zavarella, Vanni, 68